THE ROUTLEDGE
HISTORICAL ATLAS
OF THE
AMERICAN RAILROADS

THE ROUTLEDGE
HISTORICAL ATLAS
OF THE
AMERICAN RAILROADS

JOHN F. STOVER

MARK C. CARNES, SERIES EDITOR

ROUTLEDGE

NEW YORK AND LONDON

Published in 1999 by
Routledge
29 West 35th Street
New York, NY 10001

Published in Great Britain in 1999 by
Routledge
11 New Fetter Lane
London EC4P 4EE

Text Copyright © 1999 by John F. Stover
Maps and design © 1999 by Arcadia Editions Ltd.

Printed in the United Kingdom on acid-free paper.

10 9 8 7 6 5 4 3 2 1

Library of Congress Cataloging-in-Publication Data

Stover, John F.
    The Routledge historical atlas of the American railroads :
Routledge atlases of American history / John F. Stover.
      p. cm. — (Routledge atlases of American history)
    Includes bibliographical references and index.
    ISBN 0-415-92134-1 (cloth : acid free paper). — ISBN
0-415-92140-6 (paper : acid free paper)
    1. Railroads—United States—History—Maps. I. Title.
II. Title: Historical atlas of the American railroads. III. Series.
G1201.P3 S8 1999 <G&M>
385'. 0973'022—DC21   99–27356
                                                CIP
                                                MAPS

For Robert Vernon Stover

CONTENTS

FOREWORD 8

Time and Distance—Travel in 1800 10

American Railroads in the Early 1830s 12

Some Problems Solved 14

A Broken Skein of Lines 16

The Travels of Abe Lincoln, 1849 and 1861 18

Major Developments in the 1850s 20

Western Commercial Traffic Changes Direction 22

The Speed of Travel in 1860 24

Gauge Differences in 1860 26

Railroads and the Civil War 28

Federal Land Grants for Railroads 32

Railroads to the Pacific 34

Postwar Construction 36

Troubles in the 1870s 38

A Decade of Record Railroad Building 40

God's Time Became Vanderbilt's Time 44

The Grange and the Railroads 46

The 1890s 48

Major Rail Combinations in the 1900s 50

1916: A Record Year 52

Competition for the Railroad 56

Streamliners in the 1930s 58

Another War Won 60

American Railroads in 1950 62

Baltimore & Ohio Railroad 64

Pennsylvania Railroad 66

New York Central Railroad 68

Erie Railroad 70

Southern Railway 72

Louisville & Nashville Railroad 74

Illinois Central Railroad 76

Atlantic Coast Line Railroad 78

Seaboard Air Line Railroad 80

Chesapeake & Ohio 82

Norfolk & Western 84

Union Pacific 86

Southern Pacific 88

Santa Fe 90

Northern Pacific 92

Great Northern 94

Chicago, Burlington & Quincy 96

Chicago, Rock Island & Pacific 98

Chicago & North Western 100

Chicago, Milwaukee, St. Paul & Pacific 102

New York, New Haven & Hartford 104

Missouri Pacific 106

Gulf, Mobile & Ohio 108

Missouri, Kansas & Texas 110

Denver & Rio Grande Western 112

New York, Chicago & St. Louis 114

Midcentury Problems 116

Amtrak and Conrail, Courtesy of Uncle Sam 120

The Staggers Rail Act of 1980 124

Railroads in the 1990s 126

CHRONOLOGY 130

FURTHER READING 134

INDEX 138

ACKNOWLEDGMENTS 144

FOREWORD

John Stover is one of the pre-eminent authorities on the history of the American railroads. He has published, in nearly each of the past five decades, a definitive book on the subject: *Railroads of the South, 1865–1900* (1955); *Life and Decline of the American Railroads* (1970); *Iron Road to the West: American Railroads of the 1850s* (1978); *History of the Baltimore and Ohio Railroad* (1987), and *American Railroads* (1997). We are pleased to add this volume to his weighty list of credits. Again he brings a sympathetic but not uncritical understanding of a subject that has long exerted a peculiarly strong hold upon the imagination.

It all began during the 1820s, when merchants of Baltimore, Charleston, and Boston and a few other port cities on the eastern seaboard solidified their hold on western hinterlands by casting railroad tracks into them. This enthusiasm for railroads quickly spread, and by 1840 the United States possessed almost 3,000 miles of track, nearly twice the total of all Europe. European visitors were astonished by the American mania for railroad construction. A Frenchman, Michel Chevalier, commented that "the Americans have railroads in the water, in the bowels of the earth, and in the air. . . . When they cannot construct a real, profitable railway from river to river, from city to city, or from State to State, they get one up, at least as a plaything or until they can accomplish something better. . ."

There were, to be sure, many critics. During a visit to America, Charles Dickens provided this vivid indictment of a locomotive: "On it whirls headlong, dives through the woods again, emerges in the light, clatters over frail arches, rumbles upon the heavy ground, shoots beneath a wooden bridge. . . dashes on hap-hazard, pell-mell, neck or nothing—on, on, on, tears the mad dragon of an engine with its train of cars; scattering in all directions a shower of burning sparks from its wood fire; screeching, hissing, yelling, panting; until at last the thirsty monster stops beneath a covered way to drink, the people cluster round, and you have time to breathe again."

Such criticisms, however, reflected a genteel sensibility very much at odds with a nation that was becoming an industrial giant. More characteristic of the age were the views of the orator Edward Everett, who described the locomotive as "a miracle of science, art, and capital, a magic power. . . by which the forest is thrown open, the lakes and rivers are bridged, and all Nature yields to man." Walt Whitman, who identified with the spirit of the American people, entitled one rhapsodic poem "To a Locomotive in Winter," in which he lauded the engine as an "emblem of motion and power." Ralph Waldo Emerson similarly commented: "Railroad iron is a magician's rod, in its power to evoke sleeping energies of land and water."

Stover goes beyond the contested symbolism of the railroad to focus on its steely reality. Thus he examines the fundamental issues of engineering: the width, grade, and turning radius of the track; the power generated by various wheel alignments and fuels; the relative efficiencies of iron and steel. He also considers the intellectual problems confronting the managers of these vast enterprises: the legal structure of the corporations; the evolution of an information system to operate them efficiently; and the standardization of conceptions of time. But at the heart of his analysis are the stories of each of the major railroads and the men who made and ran them.

Mark C. Carnes
Barnard College, Columbia University

Time and Distance—Travel in 1800

Two hundred years ago the speed of a horse was basically the maximum speed of land travel. The speed had changed very little over the centuries. The number of travel days allowed for a diplomat going between Rome and London in the first century A.D. and eighteen centuries later was roughly the same. Travel in the United States in 1800 was probably slower than in the days of Julius Caesar since Roman roads were generally superior to those in the United States.

But turnpikes or toll roads, canals, and fast steamboats were all to appear in America in the generation after the drafting of the 1787 Constitution. The 62-mile Lancaster to Philadelphia Turnpike was completed in 1794. Between 1811 and 1818 the National Road was built from Cumberland west over the mountains to Wheeling, Virginia. The hard-surfaced National, or Cumberland Road, had been paid for with federal dollars. Both Albert Gallatin and John Calhoun favored internal improvements such as better roads and more canals. Even with the new turnpikes, wagon freight rates were very high. After the War of 1812 the normal wagon freight rates averaged about thirty cents a ton-mile, and often were twice that. Actually farm produce was rarely carried overland. In 1817 wagon freight costs from Buffalo to New York City were three times the value of a bushel of wheat, and six times that of corn. Wagon freight was not fast. When a conestoga wagon traveled the ninety miles from New York City to Philadelphia in three days, it was called the "flying machine."

In the last decades of the eighteenth century several American inventors tried, without success, to harness steam power to river navigation. Once Robert Fulton's *Clermont* steamed up the Hudson River in 1807, this new mode of river transport was quickly accepted. Within a dozen years steamboats were busy on eastern rivers and bays, the Great Lakes, and many western rivers. In 1811 a steamboat reached New Orleans from Pittsburgh, and four years later upstream travel was successful with a completed trip from New Orleans to Pittsburgh. A unique feature of steamboat service was the fact that no new route or right-of-way had to be provided, thus no huge private or public investments were required. Once steamboat construction was mastered, hundreds of eager Americans were willing to build and operate the boats.

Strongly promoted by DeWitt Clinton, governor of New York, $8 million was spent between 1817 and 1825 in building the 364-mile Erie Canal from Albany to Buffalo. The Erie Canal was a great success and quickly brought fast economic growth to New York City. None of the dozens of projected American canals would ever match the traffic or economic success of the Erie. By the decades of the 1820s American travel and transport were easier and faster than those of the year 1800. But Americans still desired and needed a mode of overland transportation that was safe and cheap and unlimited in route and regularity. They did not have long to wait.

FRENCH LOUISIANA

Mississippi River

INDIANA TERRITORY

TERRITORY NORTHWEST OF THE OHIO RIVER

Vincennes

KENTUCKY

Nashville

TENNESSEE

TERRITORY SOUTH OF THE OHIO RIVER

MISSISSIPPI TERRITORY

S P A N I S H   F L O R I D A

New Orleans

N

NEW YORK

VERMONT

NEW HAMPSHIRE

M A S S A C H U S E T T S

Albany

Boston

Erie Canal

CONN.

R.I.

New York

1 week

5 days

3 days

2 days

1 day

PENNSYLVANIA

Pittsburgh

Lancaster Pike

NEW JERSEY

National Road

MARYLAND

DELAWARE

Washington D.C.

2 weeks

VIRGINIA

3 weeks

NORTH CAROLINA

Wilmington

SOUTH CAROLINA

Charleston

GEORGIA

Speed of travel, 1800

time of travel from New York City

road

Erie Canal

steamboat

0   200 km

0   200 miles

11

American Railroads in the Early 1830s

In England mines had for many decades hauled their coal in horse-drawn wagons with flanged wheels that ran on wooden or strap iron rails. George Stephenson perfected the steam locomotive, and in 1825 the 12-mile Stockton and Darlington Railway was opened, giving England the first common carrier railroad. Back in the United States, earlier in 1813 the unhappy Philadelphia inventor Oliver Evans had predicted that someday "carriages propelled by steam" would be in common use. Colonel John Stevens operated his "steam waggon," the first real locomotive in the nation, around a circle of track on his estate. A year later, Gridley Bryant used a broad-gauge tramway to move granite for the new Bunker Hill Monument. As word of more English railways crossed the Atlantic, Americans voiced many complaints about travel: Stagecoaches were slow and uncomfortable, especially if you sat in the middle "jump seats"; canals were frozen shut each winter and could not climb real hills; and steamboats ran aground or had their boilers explode!

In 1830 the five major Atlantic coastal cities—Boston, New York, Philadelphia, Baltimore, and Charleston—had varying degrees of interest in the new railroads. New York City had passed Philadelphia in population in 1810 and claimed 202,000 in 1830. Proud of the success of the Erie Canal, it boasted that nearly half of the nation's foreign trade passed through its ample harbor. Thus it had little immediate interest in building railroads. Philadelphia had decided that its future lay in the proposed 345-mile Main Line (made up chiefly of new canals) to the Ohio River. Boston was worried over the success of the Erie Canal, but was slow to embrace railroads.

Baltimore and Charleston were both eager to build railroads to the west to share in the expanding western domestic trade. Five new western and southern states had been admitted to the Union between 1816 and 1821. Baltimore's

The First Railway Train, by E. L. Henry shows the De Witt Clinton and the first trip by rail from Albany to Schenectady in 1831.

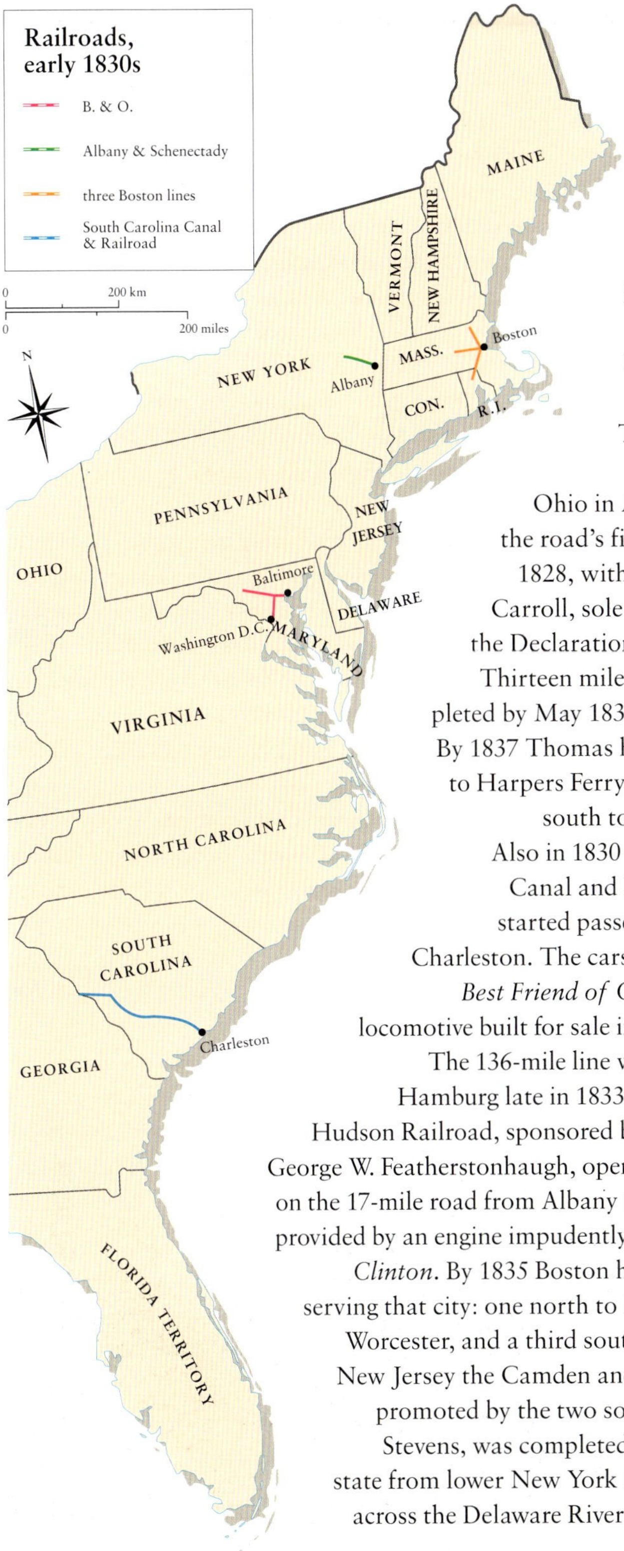

Railroads, early 1830s

- ▬ B. & O.
- ▬ Albany & Schenectady
- ▬ three Boston lines
- ▬ South Carolina Canal & Railroad

0   200 km
0   200 miles

N

MAINE

VERMONT

NEW HAMPSHIRE

NEW YORK

MASS.   Boston

Albany

CON.   R.I.

PENNSYLVANIA

NEW JERSEY

OHIO

Baltimore

DELAWARE

Washington D.C. MARYLAND

VIRGINIA

NORTH CAROLINA

SOUTH CAROLINA

Charleston

GEORGIA

FLORIDA TERRITORY

population had grown sixfold since 1790 and, with a population of 81,000 in 1830, it was the third-largest city in the country. The merchants and bankers of the city, led by Philip E. Thomas, organized the Baltimore & Ohio in April 1827 and laid the road's first stone on July 4, 1828, with the aid of Charles Carroll, sole surviving signer of the Declaration of Independence. Thirteen miles of line were completed by May 1830, to Ellicott Mills. By 1837 Thomas had pushed the line to Harpers Ferry and built a branch south to Washington, D.C. Also in 1830 the South Carolina Canal and Railroad Company started passenger service out of Charleston. The cars were pulled by the *Best Friend of Charleston*, the first locomotive built for sale in the United States. The 136-mile line was finished west to Hamburg late in 1833. The Mohawk and Hudson Railroad, sponsored by the English-born George W. Featherstonhaugh, opened in 1831. Service on the 17-mile road from Albany to Schenectady was provided by an engine impudently named the *DeWitt Clinton*. By 1835 Boston had built short lines serving that city: one north to Lowell, one west to Worcester, and a third south to Providence. In New Jersey the Camden and Amboy Railroad, promoted by the two sons of Colonel John Stevens, was completed by 1834 across the state from lower New York harbor to Camden, across the Delaware River from Philadelphia.

Some Problems Solved

The William Galloway, *an exact reproduction of the earlier* Lafayette, *and one of the first Baltimore & Ohio engines with a horizontal boiler, was acquired in the late 1830s.*

Railroads expanded quite rapidly in the decade of the 1830s, and by 1840 some sixty different lines operated a total of over 2,800 miles. Of the twenty-six states in 1840 only four (Arkansas, Missouri, Tennessee, and Vermont) lacked their first mile of track. Only nine states in the country had more than 100 miles of line. Among the states, Pennsylvania was first in mileage, New York second, and Massachusetts third. The eleven New England and mid-Atlantic states accounted for more than 70 percent of the total mileage. Southern states claimed about 600 miles, while the old Northwest had only 133 miles. The Panic of 1837 had little effect on rail construction, and much new mileage was added between 1838 and 40. Europe had about 1,500 miles of railway in 1840, which had cost more than the $75 million invested in American railroads.

Of course, there was considerable opposition as many railroads in the nation were projected and built in the decade of the 1830s. Turnpikes and canal companies, stagecoach lines, tavern keepers and timid citizens all were loud in their dissent. One Boston editor claimed a projected line to Albany would be as useless as a "railroad to the moon." Railroads running parallel to the Erie Canal had to pay tolls equal to those of the canal. A school board in Ohio called railroads "a device of Satan." Turnpike interests in Massachusetts called railroad promoters "cruel turnpike killers" and "despisers of horseflesh." It was claimed that high speed rail travel could cause "concussion of the brain." But most Americans favored the new mode of travel and agreed with a French visitor who believed the Americans had a passion for railroads.

A newspaper protest against the dreadful railroads.

Technical improvements and changes kept early railroad officials busy. Some of the early changes came in the roadbed and track. The heavy stone blocks under the track soon gave way to wooden cross ties embedded in a gravel roadbed. The thin iron strap rails on wooden track often worked loose to form "snakeheads," which caused havoc in the car floor above. Solid iron rails replaced strap rails, soon to be replaced by T-rail, introduced by Robert L. Stevens, president of the Camden and Amboy. Many American lines were built in the English 4-foot, $8^{1}/_{2}$-inch standard gauge, but southern lines often preferred a 5-foot gauge; a few northern lines also used a wider gauge.

There were also changes made in locomotives and cars. Philip E. Thomas, B&O president, soon gave up all horse power, even for the steeper grades, for steam locomotives. The first American locomotives had four drivers with a rigid front axle. In 1832 John B. Jervis, chief engineer for the Mohawk and Hudson, with some help

from Horatio Allen, built the *Experiment*, with a four-wheel swivel truck replacing the two front drivers. The new type engine could negotiate sharp curves easily and soon was widely adopted. In 1839 Henry R. Campbell of Philadelphia designed an eight-wheeled engine (a swivel truck plus four drivers). This wheel-type engine, known as the American-type locomotive, would dominate American locomotive design for the next half century. Matthias Baldwin, a Philadelphia watchmaker-merchant, built his first locomotive in the 1830s. Despite initial misgivings, he would build 1,500 engines before his death in 1866. In the 1830s and 1840s such extras as engine cabs, headlights, bells, and cow catchers were all added to early American locomotives.

The first passenger cars followed stagecoach design, but by the mid-1830s corridor type cars (a long coach with four-wheeled trucks at either end) were being introduced. Freight cars also soon had two four-wheel trucks and a load capacity of five to eight tons. Unlike canal and turnpikes, railroads owned and operated all the engines and rolling stock on their lines. As common carriers, railroads were expected to accept for shipment anything within reason.

Matthias Baldwin. When the owner of Baldwin's first locomotive complained, the disgruntled builder said, "This is our last locomotive." By the time Baldwin died in 1866 he had built 1500 more engines.

Baltimore & Ohio survey in the upper valley of the Potomac. From a painting by H. D. Stitt.

Railroads, 1840: 2,808 miles

0   200 km

0   200 miles

A Broken Skein of Lines

In the 1840s railroad building easily kept pace with the many technical changes and advances. The 1840 total of under 3,000 miles more than tripled to about 9,000 miles in 1850, with every state east of the Mississippi having at least a few miles of track. But the 9,000 miles of line were a broken skein, not a network, with many gaps, most of them west of the Appalachian Mountains.

Again the eleven New England and mid-Atlantic states, with 5,300 miles of line, had about 60 percent of the national total. Nathan Hale, longtime Boston editor, president of the Boston & Worcester, and nephew of the Revolutionary War patriot, urged that the western railroad be built on west of Worcester via Springfield and Pittsfield to Albany. When opened late in 1841 the 150-mile road connected Boston with the Erie Canal. By midcentury Massachusetts, with a thousand miles of railway, had more mileage for its area than any other state in the nation.

The Lackawanna Valley. When the youthful George Ennis painted this Scranton landscape in 1854 for the Delaware, Lackawanna & Western, the railroad president asked that three locomotives be included. For the $75 fee Innis placed only one engine in the foreground.

Four trunk lines to the west from New York City, Philadelphia, and Baltimore were planned and partially built during the 1840s. During the decade the Mohawk and Hudson, the Utica and Schenectady, and eight other short lines strung along the Mohawk Valley and the Erie Canal west to Buffalo were giving combined service to Buffalo. Later, under the leadership of Erastus Corning, nail maker and longtime Albany mayor, the ten roads merged into the New York Central. In the same years Benjamin Loder was building a broad-gauge 6-foot line diagonally across New York state from the lower Hudson River to Dunkirk on Lake Erie. In Pennsylvania John Edgar Thompson was constructing a road (later to be the Pennsylvania Railroad) from Philadelphia to Pittsburgh, and was three-quarters of the way across the state. Earlier, Thompson had built the sturdy Georgia Railroad in the South. Down in Maryland, the Baltimore & Ohio was finished well past Cumberland but was still many miles short of the Ohio River.

South of Maryland a rail network in eastern Virginia and North Carolina served Richmond and Portsmouth in Virginia and Weldon, Raleigh, and Wilmington in North Carolina. Further south, lines west from Charleston and Savannah were pushed westward to Columbia, South Carolina; Augusta and Atlanta, Georgia; and Chattanooga, Tennessee. Each of the five southern states from Kentucky south to the Gulf had only minor rail mileage. The nine southern states had a total of about 2,100 miles of railroad in 1850. The old Northwest had nearly 1,300 miles of line in 1850, with Ohio and Michigan having three-quarters of the total.

American railways in 1850 had cost perhaps $300 million to build. The total investment was about half capital stock and half bonds. At midcentury a very small portion of railroad securities were held abroad. A few states, such as

Pennsylvania, Georgia, Michigan, Indiana, and Illinois, had experimented with public construction with only minor success. The states of Massachusetts, New York, Maryland, and Virginia had provided some state assistance to several roads. The cost of construction varied from region to region. As of 1850, New England lines had cost an average of $39,000 per mile. Those in the mid-Atlantic states had cost an average of $46,000 a mile, southern roads about $24,000 a mile and those in the old Northwest about $30,000 per mile.

Railroads, 1850:
9,021 miles

The Travels of Abe Lincoln, 1849 and 1861

Abraham Lincoln took two trips between Washington, D.C., and his home in Springfield, Illinois—trips that most clearly illustrate the change in travel between the early nineteenth century and the Civil War. In 1849 he returned home from the nation's capital at the end of his single term as a congressman. Twelve years later he left Springfield for Washington, D.C., to become the nation's sixteenth President.

On a snowy March 5, 1849, a Monday, Lincoln attended the inauguration of President Zachary Taylor. Later, at an inaugural ball, he lost his hat and was forced to return bareheaded to his boarding house. Later that week he was admitted to practice law before the Supreme Court. He also applied at the Patent Office for a patent on an improved method of lifting vessels over shoals. In a few days he was packed and ready to start home to his wife. The records are sketchy, but Lincoln no doubt took the Washington branch B&O train, leaving the capital at 6:00 A.M. on either March 20 or March 21. The train connected at Relay House, seven miles west of Baltimore, with the B&O *Great Western Mail* bound for Cumberland, 178 miles west of Baltimore. The fare to Baltimore was $1.60, with another $7.00 for the ticket to Cumberland.

Arriving at Cumberland at 5:30 P.M., Lincoln would have transferred to one of several stage lines for the trip over the steep mountain grades of the National Road to Wheeling, Virginia. The 130-mile trip in a nine-passenger Concord Coach would have cost another $4.00 to $5.00 and would have entailed about twenty hours of hard travel. At Wheeling, Lincoln boarded a steamboat for the nearly 1,100-mile trip down the Ohio to Cairo and up the Mississippi to St. Louis. At midcentury, Ohio River traffic was heavy, and each week St. Louis had eight to ten arrivals from the upper Ohio. After three days on the steamboat, Lincoln reached St. Louis on March 26, 1849, and soon was home in Springfield. In 1849 Indiana had about 200 miles of railroad line, and Illinois had about 100 miles.

Three weeks before his inauguration, Lincoln left Springfield for Washington, D.C. On a rainy Monday morning, February 11, 1861, one day before his fifty-second birthday, Lincoln boarded a special train at the Great Western Railway depot in Springfield for a twelve-day trip to the nation's capital. The 1,900-mile trip was via Indianapolis, Cincinnati, Columbus, Pittsburgh, Cleveland, Buffalo, Albany, New York City, Harrisburg, Philadelphia, and Baltimore. Lincoln journeyed through eight states on over twenty different railroads.

In dozens of cities and towns, large and small, more than a million Americans heard the president-elect during the prolonged journey. The lengthy indirect trip was aimed more at creating political goodwill in a time of crisis than at assuring Lincoln a quick trip east to Washington. Lincoln could have reached Washington over several quite direct routes in well under two days, with total travel of under 1,000 miles. In 1861, seven east-west rail lines crossed the Illinois–Indiana border, another seven routes left Indiana for Ohio, and five lines went from Ohio into Pennsylvania or western Virginia. East–west rail traffic east of the upper Mississippi was abundant in 1860.

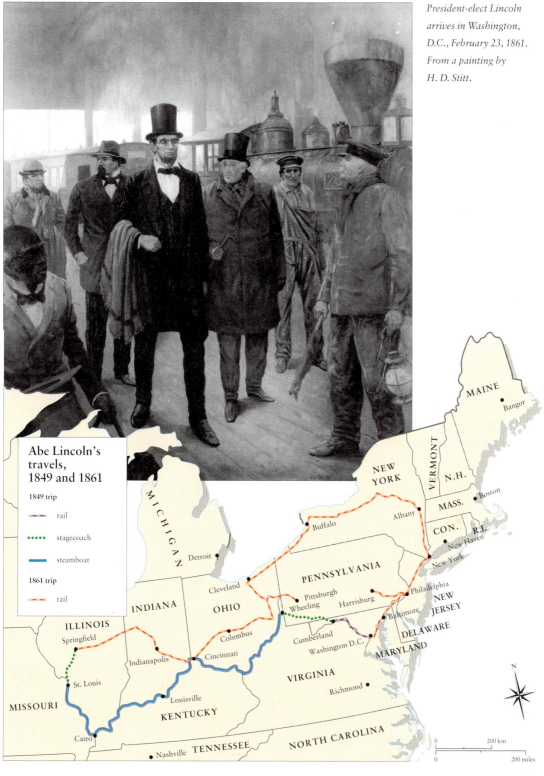

President-elect Lincoln arrives in Washington, D.C., February 23, 1861. From a painting by H. D. Stitt.

Abe Lincoln's travels, 1849 and 1861

1849 trip

━━━ rail

••••• stagecoach

━━━ steamboat

1861 trip

━━━ rail

Major Developments in the 1850s

The decade of the 1850s was one of the more dynamic periods in American railroad history. The scattered fragments of tracks at midcentury had tripled in length to grow into a network serving nearly all the populated area east of the Mississippi River. The discovery of gold in California, the promise of an expanded trans-Pacific trade, plus the new railroad land-grant policy all helped push rail construction at a rapid rate. The railroads helped expand the prosperity so typical of the 1850s.

Many railroad "firsts" appeared during the decade. The telegraph was first used to control train movement in 1851. New York City, Philadelphia, and Baltimore each reached the west between 1851 and 1852 as the Erie, the Pennsylvania, and the Baltimore & Ohio reached Dunkirk, Pittsburgh, and Wheeling. In 1856 the Illinois Central, the first railway over 700 miles in length, was completed. By the mid-fifties the United States, with no more than 5 percent of the world's population, had nearly as much rail mileage as the rest of the world. American railroads were becoming large and complex. Few other institutions in the country did business on so vast a scale or financed themselves in such a variety of ways. Not many other companies hired such numbers of men so varied in skill.

As the American rail network expanded during the decade from 9,000 miles to more than 30,000 miles, the investment in the industry grew from $300 million to $1.15 billion by 1860. The rate of growth of construction expanded unevenly across the nation. In New England, where promoters in the 1840s had overextended themselves, the increase in the 1850s was under 50 percent. Railroad building doubled in the mid-Atlantic, while southern mileage more than quadrupled. The most rapid growth in rail mileage was in the old Northwest, where the mileage increase was about eightfold for the decade.

The William Mason, *passenger locomotive built for the Baltimore & Ohio in 1856. The engine builder, William Mason, once wryly said that locomotives ought to "look better than cookstoves on wheels."*

Four trunk lines—the New York Central, the Erie, the Pennsylvania, and the Baltimore & Ohio—had completed their western lines by the mid 1850s either to Chicago or to St. Louis. By 1860 Chicago was served by eleven different railroads and was becoming the nation's leading railroad center. In 1860 Ohio was first in railroad mileage, Illinois was second, and Indiana was a strong fifth after New York and Pennsylvania.

The 30,000-mile iron network in 1860 could be divided into nearly equal thirds: 10,000 miles in the eleven-state Northeast; 11,000 in the old Northwest-Midwest; and over 9,000 miles in the South. The nearly two hundred different roads in the Northeast had a cost in 1860 of $48,000 per mile. In the Midwest the one hundred plus different roads cost $37,000 a mile to build. In the South, one hundred railroads were valued at only $28,000 per mile on the eve of the Civil War because of lighter construction, the use of slave labor, easier terrain, and lower traffic volume.

Railroads, 1860

Western Commercial Traffic Changes Direction

Since the second decade of the nineteenth century there had been a growing river traffic from the five states of the old Northwest down to New Orleans. For several decades prior to the Civil War, steamboats in the Mississippi–Ohio basin had a clear monopoly of western transportation. Thousands of westward moving settlers arrived in the West just as steamboats came to western waters. Three western states, Indiana, Illinois, and Missouri were admitted to the Union in the same years. The new canals built in Ohio and Indiana in these years helped increase the overall steamboat traffic.

Western farm crops moved south to New Orleans and the Gulf, and eastern manufactured goods moved up the Mississippi to western and northern markets. By 1850 more than six hundred steamboats of 135,000 total tons were operating on western rivers. By 1860 the number of western steamboats had climbed to over eight hundred and 196,000 tons. In the same ten years western rail mileage had grown eightfold. Most of the new rail lines ran in an east–west direction.

Steamboat freight rates were of course cheaper than railroad freight rates. In 1853 the New York Central, the Erie, and the Pennsylvania freight rates ranged from 2.4¢ to 3.5¢ per ton-mile. By 1860 these same railroads had lowered their rates to around 2¢ a ton-mile. Railroad freight rates, while higher per ton-mile than those of the steamboats, had advantage both in speed and distance. Rail routes were often shorter and more direct than river routes. The rail distance from Pittsburgh to Cincinnati was 316 miles, by river steamboat mileage was 470 miles. Steamer distance from Cincinnati to St. Louis was 702 miles, while the rail distance on the broad-gauge Ohio and Mississippi Railroad was only 339 miles. The river trip from Cincinnati to St. Louis required nearly three days—that by rail took only sixteen hours.

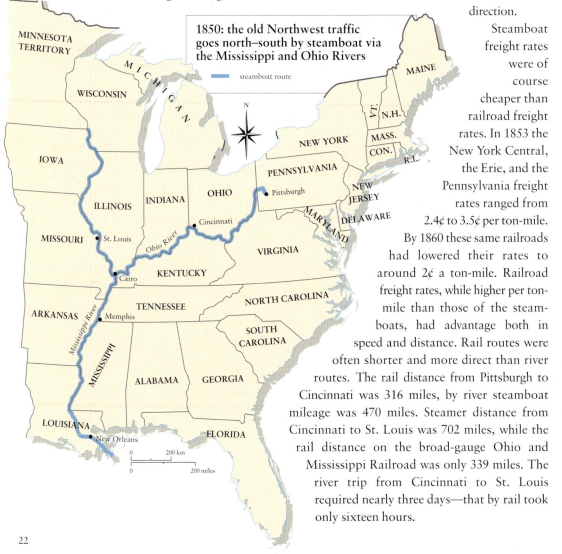

1850: the old Northwest traffic goes north–south by steamboat via the Mississippi and Ohio Rivers

—— steamboat route

The contrast between steamboat and railroad freight is well illustrated in Mark Twain's *Life on the Mississippi*: In the lush steamboat days of the 1850s the steamboat captain rations out deck space on his boat to the pleading farmer who wants to ship his wheat. Twenty years later, in the 1870s, the steamboat captain is pleading with the farmer, who is now a railroad patron, to ship by steamboat.

Between 1852 and 1856 the arrival of wheat in Chicago increased ninefold, and the comparable corn shipments quadrupled. The grain came to Chicago via the new railroads, and much of it went east the same way. Another major advantage of the railroad was its ability to enlarge the area served through the building of branch lines. Many interior towns in Ohio, Indiana, and Illinois started to grow and prosper only with the arrival of the railroad. The regular schedules of the railroad and their year-round service were other advantages over the steamboat. Often the traffic lost by steamboats in seasons of low water would be retained permanently by the railroad.

During the decade of the fifties a new east–west axis flow of traffic developed from Chicago and St. Louis east toward New York City, Philadelphia, and Baltimore. This economic alliance between the northeastern and the northwestern states was made even firmer with founding of the Republican party (a northern-only party) in the mid-1850s. The southern states may not have been fully aware of this change in traffic direction and the new east–west alliance. That a shift in trade routes had occurred is graphically made by William and Bruce Catton in their book *Two Roads to Sumter*: "Southerners who dreamed that the Northwest might be neutral or even an ally in the event of a civil conflict should have looked more closely at the endless parade of freight trains clattering across the mountains between the ocean and the Lakes."

American Express Train *(Currier and Ives print). By the years of the Civil War rail service had replaced much river traffic.*

1860: the old Northwest traffic goes east–west by railroads

Buffalo
Albany
NEW YORK
New York
PENNSYLVANIA
Pittsburgh
NEW JERSEY
Chicago
Philadelphia
Fort Wayne
OHIO
Baltimore
ILLINOIS
INDIANA
MARYLAND
DELAWARE
Cincinnati
St. Louis
MISSOURI
VIRGINIA

N

0   100 km
0   100 miles

The Speed of Travel in 1860

An artist's view of night-time travel in the late 1850s on a New York Central coach. Travel was faster but not too comfortable. (From Harper's Illustrated Weekly, *October 2, 1858.)*

By midcentury the passenger train was pushing canal packet boats and some river steam packets out of business. Even deluxe canal boats, with a top speed of 5 or 6 miles per hour, had little appeal when the steam cars could travel six times as fast. By 1860 the railroad passenger could journey from Boston to St. Louis in forty-eight hours or from New York City to Charleston in sixty-two hours. A passenger could buy a coupon rail ticket from Maine to New Orleans, check his baggage the entire distance, and note the speed performance of his train in recently available schedule books. Passenger fares in 1850 ranged from 2.5¢ to 3.5¢ a mile in the Northeast, with southern fares higher than those in the North. By the late fifties fares on many lines were down to 2¢ per mile. In 1857 the rail fare from New York City to Prairie, Wisconsin, was only $25.20. In 1859 the Erie Railroad offered tickets from New York City to Chicago for only $13.00.

Passenger cars in the 1850s were constructed of wood, with a length of about fifty feet, width of nine feet, and a capacity of fifty to sixty passengers. Illumination was provided with candles, normally one or two at each end of the car. Most cars had a toilet plus drinking water at one end of the car, a convenience rarely found on English trains. Heat was provided by a wood or coal stove. In 1859 George Pullman's sleeping car made its initial run. Dining cars were not in service in 1860—the traveler had to be satisfied with hurried meals at brief stops at railway eating houses. Many lines boasted of "on-time" performance, but Horace Greeley complained about bad connections and late trains in the North, and Frederick L. Olmsted was equally unhappy about late or slow trains in the South.

However the overall speed of travel had clearly increased since 1800. In 1800, one day's travel from New York City saw you in Philadelphia, four days in Boston or Norfolk. A week's travel in 1800 from New York City brought you to Pittsburgh, Pennsylvania, or to Wilmington, North Carolina. By 1860 a day's travel out of New York took you to Norfolk or Cleveland; in three days you could reach Florida or central Iowa; and a week's journey from New York could find you in northern Texas or eastern Nebraska.

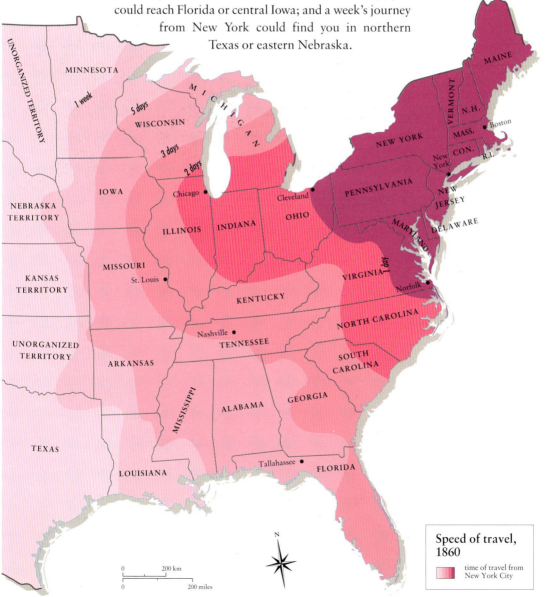

Speed of travel, 1860

time of travel from New York City

Gauge Differences in 1860

View of the Indianapolis Union Station in the late 1850s. By 1860 seven different railroads entered the city.

Western railroad construction in the 1850s had created what the historian Allan Nevins called a "web of transport" binding together the industrial-mercantile East with the agrarian West. But the web of iron rails was not tightly tied together. Major rivers had few railroad bridges, many cities did not have a physical rail connection between converging rail lines, and a variety of gauges existed throughout the total rail system.

In 1861, eight changes of cars were required on a trip between Charleston and Philadelphia. Impediments to through traffic were caused by strong local interest. Teamsters, porters, and tavern keepers were happy that not a single rail line entering either Philadelphia or Richmond made a direct connection with any other railroad entering the city. Comparable problems existed in such cities as Petersburg, Wilmington, Savannah, and Montgomery. The only railroad bridge across the Mississippi River before the Civil War was the one completed in 1856 at Rock Island–Davenport. No bridges crossed the Ohio River at Cairo, Louisville, or Cincinnati. The Baltimore & Ohio crossed the Potomac at Harpers Ferry, but no railroad bridge crossed that river at Washington, D.C.

Track gauge—the distance between the rail, measured inside to inside—varied from region to region in the nation. The 4-foot, $8^{1}/_{2}$-inch English or standard gauge was dominant in the northern states, while the 5-foot gauge was quite popular in the South. At least half a dozen different rail gauges were in use in the thirty-one states with railroads on the eve of the Civil War. Each of the six states with the greatest mileage—Ohio, Illinois, New York, Pennsylvania, Indiana, and Virginia—had at least two different gauges.

Chicago lakefront in the late 1850s. View is looking south from Randolph Street.

Fifteen states had all track in a single gauge, eight states having the standard gauge, and four southern states the 5-foot gauge. Up in Maine, John A. Poor, older brother of the editor of the *American Railroad Journal*, insisted that his Atlantic and St. Lawrence—which would make Portland the winter port for Montreal, Canada—be built in 5-foot, 6-inch Canadian gauge. In New York, Benjamin Loder built his Erie Railroad in the 6-foot gauge. The Erie also used broad 6-foot track on its branch lines in Pennsylvania and New Jersey. However most New Jersey lines still used a different 4-foot, 10-

inch gauge. The 4-foot, 10-inch gauge was also dominant in the state of Ohio. The standard 4-foot, 8½ inch gauge was the only gauge found in the three southern New England states plus Maryland, Delaware, Michigan, Wisconsin and Iowa. The 5-foot gauge was the only gauge in South Carolina, Georgia, Florida, and Tennessee, and it was dominant in three other southern states. The 5-foot, 6-inch width was found in Louisiana, Missouri, Arkansas, and Texas.

This gauge variance hurt the war effort in both the North and the South during the Civil War. The nation would not achieve a single basic gauge until the decade of the 1880s. A major result of this gauge variety, in conjunction with the lack of easy transfer facilities and the absence of major bridges, was that a long century ago nearly all freight cars belonged to the railroad on which they were running.

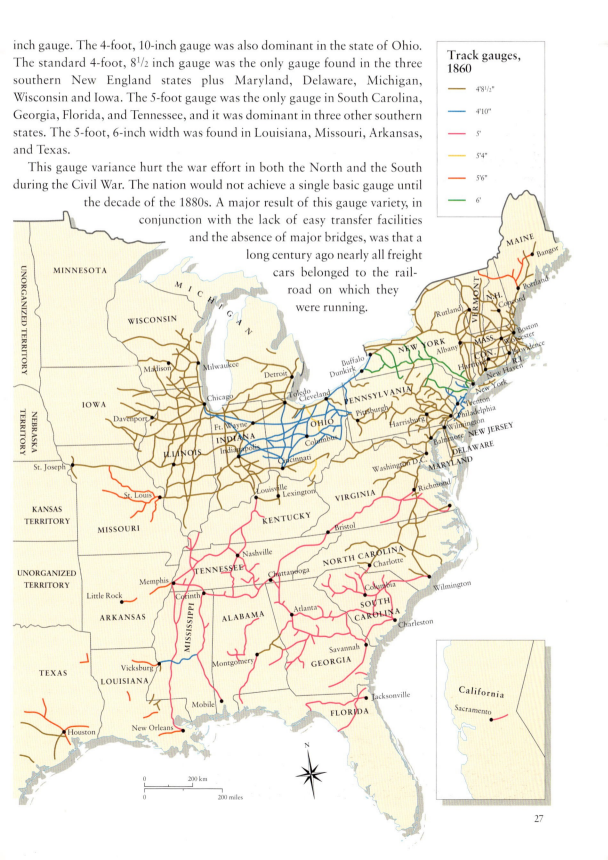

Track gauges, 1860

— 4'8½"
— 4'10"
— 5'
— 5'4"
— 5'6"
— 6'

Railroads and the Civil War

The Civil War, 1861–1865, was the first armed conflict in which railroads played a major role. As the war started, the *American Railroad Journal* stated that most railroads would not be affected by the dispute. The *Journal*'s opinion was way off the mark. Soon both Union and Confederate railroad lines were crowded with trains carrying troops and military supplies to the fronts in Virginia and Tennessee. The war brought prosperity to the railroads both in the North and the South. The New York Central paid dividends of 6 percent in 1860 that climbed to 9 percent by 1864. The operating ratio of the Petersburg Railroad in Virginia fell below 28 percent in 1862.

Confederate purchases from the North were so heavy that early in the war James Guthrie, president of the Louisville and Nashville, imposed a ten-day embargo on his line. Soon the declining value of the Confederate currency brought inflation to southern railways. Between 1861 and 1864 prices rose—lubricating oil from $1.00 to $50.00 a gallon; mechanic's wages from $2.50 to $20.00 a day; coal from 12¢ to $2.00 a bushel.

Grenville M. Dodge. Dodge, a civil engineer and surveyor, was a major general in the Civil War and chief engineer on the Union Pacific, from 1866 to 1870. Later he projected and built other railroads in the Southwest and West.

In 1861 the rival rail systems offered more in the way of contrast than comparison. The eleven Confederate states, with about 9,000 miles of road, possessed a small third of the nation's rail system. The southern railroads had been more lightly built, carried a smaller volume of traffic, and employed only a fifth of the country's railroad workers. Since many southern workers disliked mechanical pursuits, many Yankees had moved south to man southern railways. With the coming of war many of the northern railroaders returned home, and a number of those that remained in the South were viewed with suspicion.

There was a great disparity between southern and northern motive power and rolling stock. Two or three of the northern trunk lines together had as many locomotives as were in the entire Confederacy. The 142-mile Northern Central, a line in Maryland and Pennsylvania, had a roster of 42 locomotives, 38 passenger cars, and 1,455 freight cars. Virginia's 143-mile Richmond and Danville had only 22 locomotives, 20 passenger cars, and 410 freight cars.

The South was also at a difficult disadvantage both in wartime procurement and in maintenance of motive power, rolling stock, and track. For many years southern rail officials had purchased the bulk of their equipment from northern states. In the North there were a dozen locomotive plants for every one in the South. Pennsylvania by itself probably manufactured more rolling stock than the entire Confederacy. Southern states produced some iron rails, but the 26,000 tons produced in 1860 were

Railroads and the Civil War

- Union state
- border slave state
- Confederate state
- territory
- 4'8½" or 4'10" gauge railroad
- 5' gauge railroad
- Northern route
- Southern route

only a bit more than 10 percent of the northern production. English rails were not available to the South during the war because of the Northern blockade. The Tredegar Iron Works in Richmond was too busy from 1861 to 1865 meeting Confederate ordnance needs to produce many iron rails for the South. Soon southern railways were taking up rail from branch lines to maintain their principal routes.

Each side sought to destroy the railroads of the enemy, but since most of the fighting was in southern states, the Confederate losses were much greater. The worst Confederate railroad damage was during General Sherman's five-month movement through Georgia and the Carolinas in 1864–1865. The Baltimore & Ohio was the only northern road to suffer any serious damage at the hands of the Confederate forces.

Two views of Civil War railroading. Left is shown the wealth of stored rails at Alexandria, Virginia, for the U.S. Military Railroads. The scene at right is a wrecked locomotive at Richmond, Virginia, in April 1865.

During the war the Confederacy built two short connecting links of railroad, one in Virginia–North Carolina, and a second in Alabama. By 1862 a gap in the line from Meridian, Mississippi, to Selina, Alabama, was closed. The next year the Piedmont Railroad was finished from Greensboro, North Carolina, north about 40 miles to Danville, connecting with the Richmond & Danville Railroad. Both of the new roads were interior routes well away from coastal cities.

In the autumn of 1863 first the South and then the Union made major troop movements to northern Georgia and southeastern Tennessee. In mid-

September 1863 General James Longstreet's entire First Corps of the Army of Northern Virginia (12,000–15,000 men) were moved over ten railroads some 900 miles from Richmond to northern Georgia. The entire operation took only about one week. The railroads of the South were still in fair shape in 1863. Early in October 1863, Secretary of War Edwin M. Stanton proposed to President Lincoln's cabinet that 30,000 men from the Army of the Potomac be sent from the Washington area west to break the siege of Chattanooga. Stanton claimed the movement could be done in five days, but Lincoln was very skeptical. In less than twelve days 25,000 men and ten batteries of artillery, with all their horses, were moved by rail about 1,200 miles from Washington to the banks of the upper Tennessee River. The route of the thirty trains and about six hundred cars was via Harpers Ferry, Columbus, Indianapolis, Louisville, and Nashville. This long, involved trip was directed by two northern railroad officials, Vice President Tom Scott of the Pennsylvania, and President John W. Garrett of the Baltimore & Ohio.

By the spring of 1865 Confederate railroads were in a shambles. The typical southern line was a mix of twisted rails, broken engines, dilapidated cars, and gutted depots. In May 1865, when Chief Justice Salmon P. Chase toured North Carolina by rail, he was provided with a train described as a "wheezy little locomotive and an old mail car with the windows smashed and half the seats gone."

Federal Land Grants for Railroads

The movement of U.S. mail by railroad in the mid-1870s as viewed by Harper's Weekly.

Prior to 1850 the only federal aid given to American railroads consisted of several route surveys by U.S. Army engineers and a tariff reduction from 1830 to 1843 on imported iron and rails. Between 1850 and 1871 Uncle Sam offered 170 million acres of land to aid in the building of eighty odd projected railroads in central and western United States. Eventually 131 million acres would be granted in the construction of 18,738 miles of railroad, chiefly located on the frontier and beyond. The railways of Europe never enjoyed such a bounty from their several countries.

In 1850 Senators Stephen A. Douglas of Illinois and William R. King of Alabama finally pushed through Congress the first land-grant act aiding the construction of two north–south railroads. The legislation granted six alternate sections of land per mile of line to the Illinois Central in Illinois and the connecting Mobile & Ohio in the states of Mississippi and Alabama. The 700-mile Illinois Central, a wishbone shaped road from Chicago and Dunleith south to Cairo, was completed in 1856. The new road in Illinois soon was selling thousands of acres of land from its 2.5-million-acre grant on easy credit to hundreds of new settlers. The Mobile & Ohio did the same with its southern grant, but the Mobile road was finished up to Columbus, Kentucky, only in the spring of 1861. In the decade of the 1850s nearly 20 million additional acres were granted to railroads in the tier of states just west of the Mississippi, plus the states of Wisconsin, Michigan, and Florida. Grants in 1856 to Iowa provided for four east–west roads across the state. Most of the grants offered in the 1850s provided for six sections per mile of track built, with alternate sections to be sold by Uncle Sam at $2.50 per acre. In the 1850s the Illinois Central sold much of its land for $8.00 to $10.00 an acre with easy credit. Late in the 1860s much railroad land-grant acreage in Iowa sold for $7.00 to $10.00 an acre.

Like earlier congressional land grants to turnpikes and canals, the railroad land grant acts carried the phrase, "free from toll or other charge" for property or troops carried for the U.S.

Federal Land Allegedly Granted to Railroads

This map originally was published in 1884 as a Democratic campaign ad against the Republican, and was entitled *How the Public Domain has been squandered by Republican Congresses*. It exaggerated about four times the area received by the railroads.

land grant

0   300 km
0   300 miles

N

government. Later the courts decided the phrase should mean to reduce charges for government transport by 50 percent. In the Civil War years the Illinois Central carried huge Union shipments and troops south to Cairo to support General Ulysses S. Grant in his drive into the Confederacy. Even with discounted rates the Illinois Central made good profits. The railroad paid 8 percent dividends in 1863 that were raised to 10 percent in 1865.

Camel locomotive No. 65, one of many built by Ross Winans for B&O prior to the Civil War.

After the Civil War still larger land grants—of ten, twenty and even forty sections per mile of track—were offered to several projected railroads to the far Pacific. The last such grants were approved in 1871. Most of the larger grants were made by the Republicans during the years of Reconstruction. In the campaign of 1884 the Democratic Party released a map entitled: "How the Public Domain has been Squandered by Republican Congresses." The map exaggerated the true extent of the grants about four-fold by ignoring the alternate section patterns and including many indemnity lands that were to be used only if the primary strip was exhausted. The original Democratic map of 1884 was widely copied in textbooks in public schools for sixty years and was only corrected in the 1940s. Thus for two generations Americans grew up believing that 80 percent of Iowa had been given to the railroads. Even so the 131 million acres finally granted the railroads after 1850 was immense. It amounted to about 7 percent of the total land area of the contiguous United States.

President Millard Fillmore signed the first Federal Land-Grant Act on September 20, 1851.

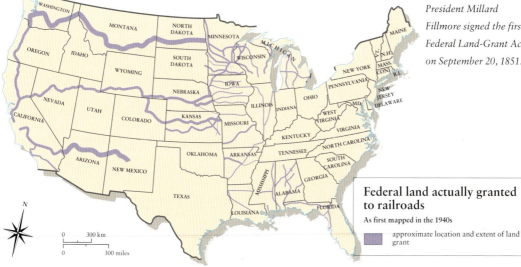

Federal land actually granted to railroads

As first mapped in the 1940s

approximate location and extent of land grant

33

Railroads to the Pacific

In 1865 the western fingers of the iron rail network were near the frontier line in Wisconsin, Iowa, Missouri, Arkansas, and Texas. West of that frontier stretched the Great Plains, or the "Great American West." This was the region that Horace Greeley described as lacking in settlement because there was so little wood and water. Instead the lonely region had plenty of land, warlike Indians, and distance. Greeley, Abraham Lincoln, and other commentators of the sixties believed it might take a century to settle this last frontier. In many railways projected for the region, the words "Pacific" or "Western" were included in the official titles. These new western railroads solved the problem of distance, bringing many settlers to the area and opening eastern markets for western farm products. Only half a century was needed for the admission of the last of the forty-eight states.

The first line to the Pacific was made possible with the passage of the Pacific Railway Bill, signed by Abraham Lincoln on July 1, 1862. The legislation stated that the line to the Pacific was to be constructed by two companies: the Union Pacific, which would build westward from the Missouri River, and the Central Pacific, which would build eastward from Sacramento, California. The Central Pacific had been organized in 1861. Both lines were to receive ten alternate sections of federal land, which was increased in 1864 to twenty sections, for each mile of track. Each railroad was also given thirty-year government loans, ranging from $16,000 to $48,000 per mile, according to the difficulty of the terrain of the route. Both roads were to be built in standard gauge.

The Union Pacific was capitalized at $100 million when organized in 1863. Dr. Thomas C. Durant was the vice president of the company, and he actively directed the project. Dr. Durant was much better known for his skill in the manipulation of capital stock than for his practice of medicine. Ground was broken for the U.P. at Omaha, Nebraska, late in 1863, but little was accomplished until after the end of the Civil War. By 1865 Dr. Durant had helped create a false-front construction company known as the Credit Mobilier that directed illegal extra profits to Union Pacific insiders. Early in 1866 General Grenville M. Dodge became chief engineer for the Union Pacific. General Dodge hired the Casement brothers, Daniel and Jack, to direct the roadwork gangs of up to ten thousand men—ex-soldiers from both armies, ex-convicts, and Irish from New York City—to build the road. In 1867 and 1868 more than 450 miles of U.P. track had been laid, and by early 1869 the end of the U.P. track was well beyond Ogden, Utah.

In the late 1860s the Central Pacific was also being built through California and Nevada by four hard-headed merchants from Sacramento: Leland Stanford, grocer and soon to be the California governor; Mark Hopkins and Collis P. Huntington, partners in a hardware store; and dry goods merchant Charles Crocker. The two roads were joined on May 10, 1869, in a golden-spike ceremony at

The giant windmill at Laramie, Wyoming Territory, supplied water for Union Pacific engines. A twenty stall roundhouse is in the background.

Promontory Point, Utah. The Credit Mobilier scandal would later affect the careers of Vice President Schuyler Colfax, Speaker James G. Blaine, and President James A. Garfield. The Central Pacific also profited from false-front construction operations but suffered a fire that destroyed company records.

In later years the Union Pacific would complete major branch lines such as the Kansas Pacific, the Denver Pacific, and lines

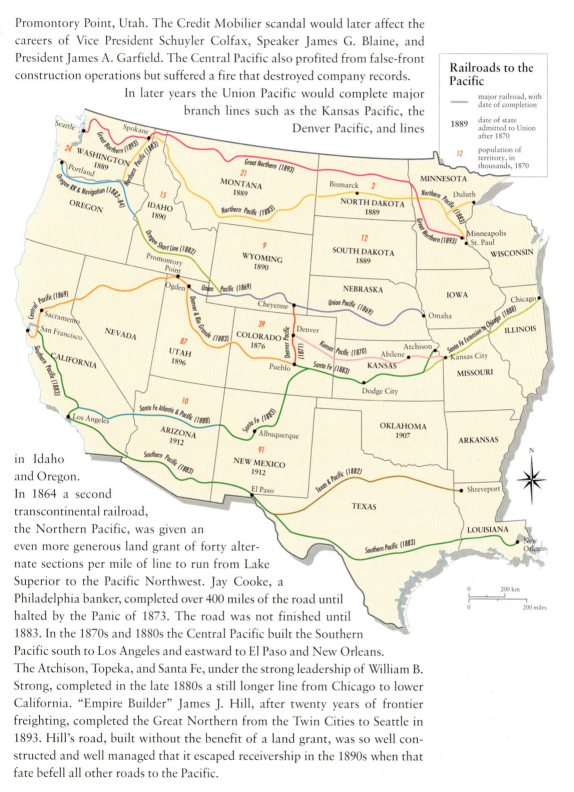

Railroads to the Pacific

——	major railroad, with date of completion
1889	date of state admitted to Union after 1870
12	population of territory, in thousands, 1870

in Idaho and Oregon.

In 1864 a second transcontinental railroad, the Northern Pacific, was given an even more generous land grant of forty alternate sections per mile of line to run from Lake Superior to the Pacific Northwest. Jay Cooke, a Philadelphia banker, completed over 400 miles of the road until halted by the Panic of 1873. The road was not finished until 1883. In the 1870s and 1880s the Central Pacific built the Southern Pacific south to Los Angeles and eastward to El Paso and New Orleans. The Atchison, Topeka, and Santa Fe, under the strong leadership of William B. Strong, completed in the late 1880s a still longer line from Chicago to lower California. "Empire Builder" James J. Hill, after twenty years of frontier freighting, completed the Great Northern from the Twin Cities to Seattle in 1893. Hill's road, built without the benefit of a land grant, was so well constructed and well managed that it escaped receivership in the 1890s when that fate befell all other roads to the Pacific.

Postwar Construction

Test of the George Westinghouse Air Brake. In the spring of 1869, an unexpected test of the new brake came when a Pennsylvania Railroad train equipped with the brake unexpectedly nearly hit a horse-drawn wagon. The brake worked perfectly.

Even with four years of war, American rail mileage had climbed by 73 percent in the decade of the 1860s, up to 52,900 miles by 1870. The first half of the decade saw about 4,000 miles built, most of it in the north and west. During the four years of the war the Confederacy had actually lost mileage. The total gain of 22,000 miles in the decade varied greatly from region to region. The 800 miles built in New England produced an increase of 23 percent, while the 4,200 new miles in the five mid-Atlantic states gave an increase of 66 percent. In the South (the Confederacy plus Kentucky and West Virginia) the 3,000 miles of new track meant a 31 percent gain. The Old Northwest, with 5,000 new miles, gained 54 percent. Other states beyond the Mississippi claimed nearly 11,000 miles in 1870 or a sevenfold increase over the 1860 figure of 1,500 miles. States with the greatest mileage were Illinois, Pennsylvania, New York, Ohio, and Indiana.

During the decade several small but still important changes showed the growing maturity of American railroading. During the Civil War the combined freight tonnage of the Erie and the New York Central lines for the first time exceeded that of the Erie Canal. In 1862 a trial postal car for the sorting of mail en route was used in Missouri on the Hannibal and St. Joseph line. In 1863 dining-car service was introduced on a route between Baltimore and Philadelphia. In 1865 the first horizontal oil-tank car was placed in service. In the same year steel rails were being produced in the nation, but the railroad industry was slow to order the new type of rail. By the late 1862 "cooperative" fast freight service began to appear in which several railroads would club together and furnish cars for long-distance freight service over the tracks of the several roads. The new service was faster and offered shippers through bills of lading. In 1868 Eli H. Janney received a patent for his automatic coupler to replace the older "link-and-pin" coupler. George Westinghouse in 1869 applied for a patent for an automatic air-brake. Neither of the two new devices were to be quickly accepted by American railroads.

During the 1860s Commodore Cornelius Vanderbilt, after six decades with both sail- and steamboats, turned to railroads. In 1862 he purchased a controlling interest in both the New York and Harlem and the New York and Hudson lines, which provided service up the Hudson to Albany. At Albany the New York Central, headed by Erastus Corning, transferred the passengers and freight to Vanderbilt's roads only when the Hudson was frozen and the steamboats were tied up for the season. The Commodore was not very happy with this routine. Corning retired in 1864, and the current manager soon capitulated to the Commodore. In January 1867, in the depth of winter, Vanderbilt suddenly stopped taking New York Central freight and passengers from the New York Central down to New York City. Before the end of 1867 Vanderbilt was in full control of the New York Central, giving him through service from New York City to Buffalo.

Railroads, 1870:
52,922 miles

Troubles in the 1870s

The rapid expansion of railroads in the late 1860s continued into the next decade, increasing from 52,900 miles in 1870 to 93,200 miles in 1880, an increase of 76 percent. New England rail mileage climbed 32 per-

B&O bosses at Grafton, West Virginia, in 1871.

cent during the 1870s, while that in the mid-Atlantic region rose by 42 percent. The total mileage of 19,000 in the South was 55 percent above the 1870 figure, while the 25,000 miles in the old Northwest in 1880 was 70 percent above that of a decade before. The western states and territories climbed from 11,000 miles in 1870 to 27,500 in 1880, an increase of 151 percent. By 1880 every one of the 48 states, or states to be, had at least some railway mileage. The mileage ranking was identical to that of 1870 except that Iowa replaced Indiana for fifth place.

In the first years of the decade the pace of building was hectic—in 1871, 1872, and 1873 over 17,000 miles of track were laid, an average of nearly 5,800 miles a year. The failure of the banker Jay Cooke and the Panic of 1873 brought a drastic change. In the South more than two-fifths of the railroads were in default or receivership. In the rest of the country a quarter of the roads were in default. As a result only 11,500 miles of new line were built in the five years from 1874 to 1878——less than 2,300 miles a year.

In 1874 the rotund John W. Garrett, president of the Baltimore & Ohio, completed his road to Chicago. Garrett declared that, like the biblical Samson, he would pull down the temple of high freight rates upon the heads of rival lines. Rate wars were quite common in the seventies among the B&O, the New

York Central, and the Pennsylvania. Vanderbilt once lowered livestock rates from Buffalo to New York City to $1.00 a head. At once the clever Jim Fisk bought cattle in Buffalo and shipped them profitably to New York City at his rival's expense. Rate wars generally ended when the trunk line presidents, Vanderbilt, Garrett, and Tom Scott or Thompson of the Pennsylvania met at a resort such as Saratoga in upstate New York to make their peace and raise their rates. Shippers benefited from the fact that the new, stabilized rates generally were a bit lower than the level of rates prior to the rate wars. Average freight rates dropped from about 2¢ a ton-mile in 1865 to 0.75¢ by 1900.

Labor violence came with the Railroad Strike of 1877. The Big Four Brotherhoods had already started to organize: engineers in 1863, conductors in 1868, firemen in 1873 and trainmen in 1883. Early in 1877 most eastern lines reduced wages by 10 percent. When the B&O cut their wages another 10 percent in July the angry B&O crews went out on strike. The strike quickly spread to Pittsburgh, Chicago, St. Louis, and Omaha. Federal troops finally broke the strike but only after thirty people were killed and $5,000,000 worth of property was lost, much of it in Pittsburgh.

Interior of a Rock Island diner in the 1870s.

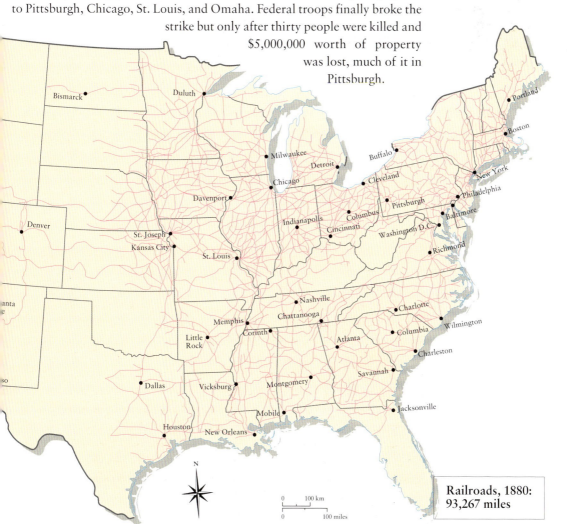

Railroads, 1880:
93,267 miles

A Decade of Record Railroad Building

Railroad construction in the 1880s increased at the same rate, 76 percent, as it had in the previous decade. The record was not the rate of increase, but rather the actual miles built: from 93,200 miles of track in 1880 to 163,600 miles by the end of 1889, gain of 70,400 miles. Average annual construction was 7,000 miles. The lowest year, 1885, had only 3,600 miles built, while in 1887 nearly 12,000 miles were added to the national rail system. The ten years included the four highest construction years in American railroad history: 1881, 1882, 1886, and 1887.

The new construction was mainly in the south and the west. New England mileage increased only by one-seventh, mid-Atlantic states by less than one-third, and the old Northwest climbed less than one-half. The southern states, south of the Ohio and the Potomac and east of the Mississippi, saw an increase of 98 percent, while rail mileage west of the Mississippi grew by 129 percent. The states with the greatest total mileage in 1890, in order of rank, were Illinois, Kansas, Texas, Pennsylvania, and Iowa. Three of the five were west of the Mississippi, and only one was in the East. A major reason for great increase in building was that the decade was generally prosperous, lacking the major depressions of the 1870s and 1890s.

During the 1880s American railroads finally achieved a uniformity of gauge by accepting the standard 4-foot, 8½-inch gauge. During the sixties and seventies several expedients had been tried—extra wide 5-inch treads on car wheels, or car axles with wheels that could be made to slide along the axle—without success. Car hoists or elevating machines had been tried with no more success. Clearly there was no substitute for the complete adoption of standard gauge for the entire country.

Slowly the odd gauges started to shift to standard. The 340-mile Ohio and Mississippi, from Cincinnati to St. Louis, shifted from 6-foot to standard gauge in 1871. In Maine, the Atlantic and St. Lawrence made the change from 5-foot, 6-inch gauge in 1874. The Erie, with its broad 6-foot gauge, shifted to standard gauge between 1878 and 1880 under the urging of Hugh Jewett, its new president. By 1880 both New Jersey and Ohio had changed their 4-foot, 10-inch gauge lines to standard. In the South the 5-foot gauge trackage had increased from 7,300 miles in 1865 to 12,000 miles by 1880, but a reversal would soon develop. In July 1881 the Illinois Central shifted its 5-foot gauge, 547-mile line from Cairo to New Orleans to standard gauge. The Mobile & Ohio did likewise in July 1885 with its 5-foot gauge.

The crusty and capable Milton Hannibal Smith, longtime Louisville & Nashville president, convinced his fellow southern top railroad officials it was time for the South to fall in line. In two days—May 31 and June 1—1886, track gangs of three to five men per mile changed 13,000 miles of 5-foot gauge to 4-foot, 9-inch gauge. This was the gauge of the Pennsylvania, the northern line most frequently exchanging cars with southern railroads. In the next few years all roads with a 4-foot, 9-inch gauge narrowed their track by half an inch to the official standard gauge, as required by the American Railway Association.

Railroads, 1890: 163,597 miles

In the early 1870s, at about the same time that the Ohio & Mississippi and the Atlantic & St. Lawrence were shifting to standard gauge, a mania for narrow-gauge railroads was developing in England. Robert F. Fairlie, an Englishman, was convinced that a railroad built in the gauge of 3 feet, 6 inches was the "Railway of the Future." He argued that the narrower gauge, which allowed smaller engines and rolling stock, would be cheaper to build and operate, with a savings of a third below a standard-gauge railroad. He believed that the sharper curves and lighter, smaller rolling stock would be ideal for mountain railroading.

By the early 1870s many Americans were starting to build narrow-gauge lines in the United States. A few lines were as narrow as the 2-foot gauge, but 95 percent of the American efforts were the 3-foot gauge. Narrow gauge railroading received a major boost when General William Jackson Palmer built his Denver & Rio Grande in the 3-foot gauge. Soon branches of Palmer's road were built to Aspen, Durango, Silverton, and northern New Mexico. By 1877 the nation had 2,850 miles of narrow-gauge lines in eighty railways in twenty-six states. Colorado had the most narrow-gauge mileage, but it was also popular in California, Nevada, and Utah. East of the Mississippi, Ohio, Pennsylvania, and Illinois each had more than 200 miles.

By 1885 over 11,500 miles of narrow-gauge line was in service in the nation. By this time much of the Denver & Rio Grande had added a third outside rail to its major routes to accommodate standard-gauge cars. By 1916 only 4,500 miles of narrow gauge was in service, and this figure had dropped to 900 miles by 1950. About two-thirds of all narrow-gauge mileage has been shifted to standard-gauge and one-third totally abandoned. In the 1990s a couple of short narrow-gauge lines in Colorado and New Mexico welcome tourist traffic.

With gauge uniformity nationwide, an early dividend was the more extensive interchange of freight cars among all the railways. For several years a rental system, at the rate of 75¢ per car mile for a "foreign" car, was in use. When railroads abused the system by using foreign cars for storage, a per diem system was put into effect. In 1902 a per diem of 20¢ a day was adopted. With inflation this rate was up to $1.00 a day in 1920 and up to $2.80 a day by 1959.

More bridges over major rivers were built after the Civil War. In 1865 the Chicago & Northwestern built a second Mississippi River bridge at Clinton, Iowa. In 1868 the Illinois Central built a bridge to the north at Dubuque, and in the same year another bridge was built at Burlington, Iowa, by the Chicago, Burlington & Quincy. In 1874 James B. Eads completed his bridge at St. Louis. Bridges across the Missouri were built at Kansas City in 1869 and at Omaha in 1871. Both Louisville and Cincinnati finished bridges over the Ohio in 1870. Various legal disputes with Kentucky delayed the efforts of the Illinois Central to bridge the Ohio at Cairo. Finally in October 1889 a $3 million, 4,600-foot, 12-span bridge was opened at Cairo. Nine 75-ton Mogul locomotives in tandem tested the 518-foot twin span. I.C. President Stuyvesant Fish and Vice

President Edward H. Harriman were behind the regular engine crew in the leading Mogul engine.

In the 1880s most trains were plagued with a pair of devices—the link-and-pin coupler and the hand brake—that made the life of every brakeman both miserable and hazardous. The link-and-pin coupler was located in such a way that the brakeman had to stand between the cars to couple them. A brakeman's occupation was easily told by a crippled hand or missing fingers. Manual braking at night on top of a car in rain or snow was equally hard on life and limb.

Major Eli H. Janney, a Confederate veteran, had invented and improved an automatic coupler. In the early 1870s he was selling the coupler, but few railroads were interested. George Westinghouse had about the same luck with his air brake, patented in 1869 and improved in 1872. Commodore Vanderbilt rebuffed the young inventor with, "Do you pretend to tell me that you could stop trains with air?" Demonstrations proved the effectiveness of the brake, but few orders appeared. In the mid-1880s Lorenzo S. Coffin, railroad commissioner for Iowa, took up the cause for railroad safety and succeeded by having Iowa pass legislation requiring all trains in the state to use air brakes and automatic couplers. Finally federal legislation in 1893 required all trains in the nation to be equipped with the new devices.

Several improvements in passenger service appeared in the 1880s. Steam heat for passenger cars was first introduced in 1881. Early in 1887 the first solid vestibule train (replacing the open platform cars) was placed in service between New York City and Chicago. Several passenger trains fully equipped with electric lights were also put into service during 1887.

B&O workers, at Grafton, West Virginia, in 1885.

God's Time Became Vanderbilt's Time

In the same decade in which the nation gained uniformity in track gauge the country also achieved standard time. In the early days of railroads no time-tables existed and depot agents had to manage with crude schedule sheets. As the iron network expanded, railroad officials ran their trains with a crazy-quilt pattern of dozens of different local sun times. When it was high noon in Chicago it was 11:27 A.M. in Omaha, 11:41 A.M. in St. Paul, 11:50 A.M. in St. Louis, 12:31 P.M. in Pittsburgh, and 12:50 P.M. in Washington, D.C. The Buffalo depot had three different clocks, each for a different railroad. A Chicago news-paper claimed that Illinois had twenty-seven different times, Wisconsin thirty-eight, and Indiana twenty-three.

On the Baltimore & Ohio, local Baltimore time was used for eastern trains, Columbus time for Ohio trains, and the Vincennes clock for all movement west of Cincinnati. The Union Pacific ran its extensive systems with six local sun times. There was a general agreement that the large railroads ran their trains on fifty-four different local times. A traveler on a journey from Maine to San Francisco might change his watch eighteen or twenty times. In Kansas City the leading jewelers furnished "standard" time with a varia-

Standard Time Zones, 1883

- Pacific Time
- Mountain Time
- Central Time
- Eastern Time

tion of up to twenty minutes until one jeweler with a single "time ball," which dropped each noon, provided a uniform time.

The Railroad Gazette in 1870 urged that the nation follow the English pattern, with a single standard time for the entire country, but that idea received little support. There was a certain desire for a program of several broad time zones for the nation, as suggested by Professor C. F. Dowd, the principal of a young ladies seminary in New York State. In 1872 a group of railroad superintendents meeting in St. Louis organized the Time Table Convention, later in 1875 called the General Time Convention.

William F. Allen, managing editor of the *Official Guide of the Railways*, became secretary of the General Time Convention in 1876. Allen at once began to work and plan for a nationwide system of four time zones: Eastern, Central, Mountain, and Pacific. By 1881 he had devised a plan of standard time zones on the 75th, 90th, 105th, and 120th meridians respectively, near the cities of Philadelphia, Memphis, Denver, and Fresno. The railroads accepted Allen's plan in 1883, with the program for standard time in four zones, to go into effect at noon on Sunday, November 18, 1883.

The public generally accepted the new railroad standard time zones, but not without some complaint. An Indianapolis newspaper said that people would marry and die on railroad time, and that preachers would preach on railroad time. As the time shift occurred, people in the eastern half of the zones would experience a "day of two noons," while those in the western half would abruptly be thrown into the future. Some complained they preferred to live in "God's time," not "Vanderbilt's time." Down in Tennessee the good Reverend Mr. Watson from his pulpit blamed the Louisville & Nashville for the new time and, to make a point, used a hammer to smash his shiny Waterbury watch. In Washington, D.C., the attorney general said some days before November 18th that no government agency had to follow the new time. There were rumors that on Sunday the 18th, that same official missed his afternoon train to Philadelphia by some eight minutes. Congress officially adopted the railroad standard time some thirty-five years later, in 1918.

The Grange and the Railroads

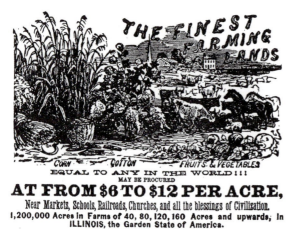

THE FINEST FARMING LANDS

CORN   COTTON   FRUITS & VEGETABLES

EQUAL TO ANY IN THE WORLD!!!
MAY BE PROCURED

AT FROM $6 TO $12 PER ACRE,

Near Markets, Schools, Railroads, Churches, and all the blessings of Civilization.
1,200,000 Acres in Farms of 40, 80, 120, 160 Acres and upwards; in
ILLINOIS, the Garden State of America.

An 1867 Illinois Central advertisement for its land-grant acres. The railroad promised high yields.

In the generation after the Civil War four prairie railroads in the Midwest were of particular importance to the farmers in the Granger area. Each of the four had been aided by federal land grants. The four Granger railroads were the Chicago, Burlington & Quincy; the Chicago, Milwaukee & St. Paul; the Chicago & North Western; and the Chicago, Rock Island & Pacific. These four railroads served the nine states from Illinois, Missouri and Kansas north to Canada (the six states to the north being Wisconsin, Iowa, Minnesota, Nebraska, North and South Dakota). Seven of these grain-growing states were west of the Mississippi, while two were to the east. All of the states and the four railroads were economically drawn to Chicago, and to some lesser extent to St. Louis, the Twin Cities, and Omaha. The four railroads in 1890 had a combined mileage of about 18,000 miles, about a third of the 1890 total for the nine-state area. The four lines in the years after the Civil War had been earning huge revenues for carrying grain, beef, and pork to the elevators and stockyards of Chicago. Each of the four railroads had been paying good dividends.

But the farmers in the Granger area had some complaints about their railroad service. A major abuse was the long- and short-haul rate discrimination. The grain rate was 12.5¢ per hundred pounds to be hauled from the Twin Cities to Chicago, while a shorter haul from a Minnesota town to St. Paul was twice as much. In 1870 grain hauled from the Mississippi to Chicago cost 20¢ a bushel, while the 700-mile haul from Chicago to the East Coast was only 40¢. It was a rare small town that had more than one railroad, and railroads liked to "charge all the traffic will bear." Almost continuously from 1870 to 1884 the Burlington, the North Western, and the Rock Island maintained the "Iowa Pool," charging farmers high rates and then splitting the revenue three ways. Farmers also complained about private and railroad-owned elevators that downgraded their grain or held their grain until a price rise came along. Other farmer charges were against the free railroad passes given Congressmen, state and local officials, judges, assessors, and members of the press. Grangers were also upset by the special rates or rebates given to large shippers. A long generation later Frederick Logan Paxson, a historian of the frontier, pointed out that for the western farmer transportation was a tax, a tax he could not avoid.

In 1867 the National Grange of the Patrons of Husbandry was organized by Oliver H. Kelley, a clerk in the Bureau of Agriculture in Washington, D. C. At first the Grange had only social and educational objectives, but the hard times of the 1870s shifted its interest to economic and political issues. The Grange had grown to 800,000 members in 20,000 local Granges by 1875. In their

Grange Halls the members could see a colored lithograph with eight men and the following captions: "I pray for all," said the parson; "I trade for all," said the merchant; "I plead for all," said the lawyer; "I legislate for all," said the statesman; "I prescribe for all," said the physician; "I fight for all," said the soldier; "I carry for all," said the railroad owner; and in the center stood the farmer, who said, "And I PAY for ALL." The western Granger farmer was tired of paying in the 1870s.

Grange-sponsored legislation creating local and statewide railroad regulation appeared in Illinois in 1871; in Iowa and Wisconsin in 1874; and in Nebraska, Kansas, and Missouri in the late 1870s. The early Grange state railroad regulations at first applied only to intrastate rail operations. Later they were extended to cover interstate commerce beyond the state borders. At first the United States Supreme Court upheld such regulations, but in the 1886 *Wabash* case the earlier opinion was reversed by the Supreme Court. In 1887 the Interstate Commerce Act passed by Congress provided for the first federal railroad regulation. A positive regulation of American railroads was thus established, regulation that would last for a century.

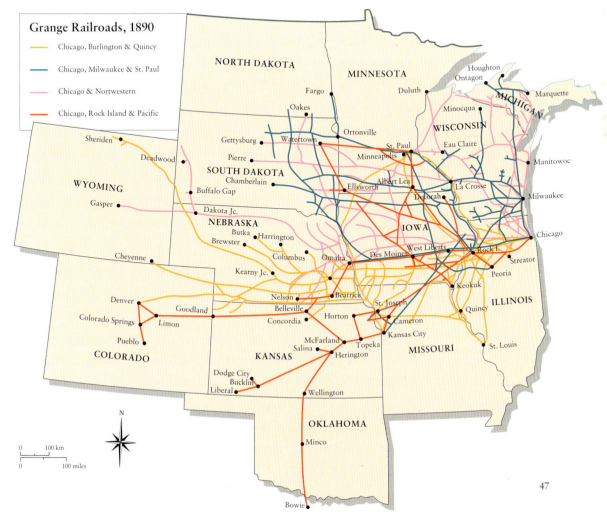

Grange Railroads, 1890

- Chicago, Burlington & Quincy
- Chicago, Milwaukee & St. Paul
- Chicago & Nortwestern
- Chicago, Rock Island & Pacific

The 1890s

In the 1890s railroad construction slowed from the hectic pace of the preceding decade. Just under 30,000 miles of new line were built in the ten years to reach a total of over 193,000 miles at the turn of the century. In 1900 only four states—Delaware, Nevada, Oklahoma, and Rhode Island—had less than a thousand miles of railroad line. It seemed to

World's Fair Crowd in 1893. Fair crowd at 63rd Street I.C. station waiting to return to downtown Chicago. At 10¢ a trip the Illinois Central grossed $800,000 during the year.

many Americans that railroads had been built into every little valley in the nation.

In the first few years of federal railroad regulation by the newly formed Interstate Commerce Commission, delayed hearings and court appeals had slowed the process, and few real changes in rail operations had developed. Many railway officials tended to agree with Richard S. Olney, a corporation attorney, who wrote of the ICC Act, "It satisfied the popular clamour for a government supervision of the railroads, at the same time that such a supervision is almost entirely nominal." In a few years that supervision would be much more than nominal.

The depression that followed the Panic of 1893 pushed many railroads into default or receivership. Soon 40,000 miles of line—or more than a fifth of the total, representing about $2.5 billion of capital—were in trouble. Seven major lines were in difficulty: the Erie; Baltimore and Ohio; Northern Pacific; Reading; Richmond and Danville; Santa Fe; and Union Pacific. Many other smaller lines were also in financial trouble. J. P. Morgan and his bank reorganized several of the roads in distress, the most important of which was the Richmond and Danville. That road, combined with the several lesser lines, was reorganized in 1894 as the Southern Railway, a 6,000-mile system serving most of the southern states.

Also in 1894 the Pullman Strike affected rail service in the Chicago area and to some extent in the rest of the country. Workers at the Pullman Palace Car Company struck in the spring of 1894. Their wages had been cut about 25 percent, without any reduction in the rent they paid for their company-owned houses. Members of the American Railway Union, recently organized by Eugene V. Debs, struck in sympathy with the Pullman workers and refused to service any trains that contained Pullman cars. Federal troops were ordered in to protect the U. S. mail, and the strike was eventually broken. Union members who were active leaders in the strike were blacklisted and given service letters with a secret watermark showing a crane with a broken neck.

In the last years of the century there was a marked increase in the use of steel rail. In 1880 about a quarter of the track rail was steel, by 1890 it was up to 80 percent, and nearly all was steel by 1900. In 1893 the New York Central locomotive *No. 999* attained a speed of 112.5 miles per hour. Two years later the first electric locomotive was put in service in Baltimore by the Baltimore & Ohio Railroad. By 1900 the average freight rate for the nation was about 0.8¢ per ton-mile, and the average passenger fare was about 2.5¢ per passenger-mile.

Railroads, 1900:
193,346 miles

Major Rail Combinations in the 1900s

The railroad reorganizations of the mid-1890s were necessary to solve the problems of the Panic of 1893 and generally led to more rail mergers and consolidations. As a result by the early years of the twentieth century seven major railroad systems or groups had appeared. J. P. Morgan had not only formed the new Southern Railway, but he had also reclaimed the Erie from receivership. Thus by the early twentieth century his bank controlled about 18,000 miles of rail property. The Vanderbilt Roads (22,000 miles) included the New York Central and the Chicago and North Western. For many years the New York Central had the charming lawyer Chauncey Depew as board chairman. The Pennsylvania Group (20,000 miles) was created in 1900 when Alexander Cassatt, president of the Pennsylvania, acquired a major share of the capital stock of both the B & O and the C & O lines. James J. Hill added the Northern Pacific to his Great Northern by 1900, and then added the Burlington in 1906 for a total of 21,000 miles. The E. H. Harriman Roads (25,000 miles) had by 1901 added both the U. P. and the S. P to his earlier controlled Illinois Central. The son of Jay Gould, George Gould, controlled 17,000 miles consisting of the Missouri Pacific and other southwestern roads. With holding company operations, the Diamond Match King, William H. Moore, built a 15,000-mile system out of the Rock Island plus other smaller properties. These seven groups made up a total of 138,000 miles out of a 1906 national total of 224,000 miles.

Edward H. Harriman. In the early twentieth century, Harriman controlled 25,000 miles of railroads, including the Illinois Central, the Union Pacific, and the Southern Pacific. He failed to acquire the Burlington.

The more restrictive federal railroad regulations that appeared in the early twentieth century resulted from several forces: first, the seven major rail groups, which were fresh evidence of railroad monopoly that added strength to earlier charges of corruption and rate discrimination; second, the appearance on the political scene of the Progressive Movement and its desire for reform; and third, the new occupant in the White House, the energetic Teddy Roosevelt, who wished to show the railroads who was in charge. In 1903 Roosevelt signed the Elkins Act, which strengthened the prohibition on railroad rebates. The railroads themselves were happy to be rid of rebates.

Three years later, in 1906, Congress passed the Hepburn Act. This legislation enlarged the ICC from five to seven members and gave the Commission the power to regulate express, pipeline, and sleeping car companies as well as railroads. The Hepburn Act also abolished the granting of passes and empowered the commission to establish "just and reasonable railroad rates." James J. Hill did not like the new regulations and wrote, "It seems hard that we should be compelled to fight for our lives against the political adventurers who have never done anything except pose and draw a salary."

William Howard Taft, who became president in 1909, had never had any great love for railroads. Shortly before his presidency he had written that they were monopolies run by eight or nine men "exceedingly lawless in spirit." The Mann-Elkins Act of 1910 further increased the power of the ICC. This act permitted the commission to suspend new rates for as long as ten months, and the burden of proof as to the reasonableness of new rates was placed upon the railroad, not the shipper. By 1910 the

regulation of railroads was no longer just the "nominal" regulation Richard Olney described in 1892.

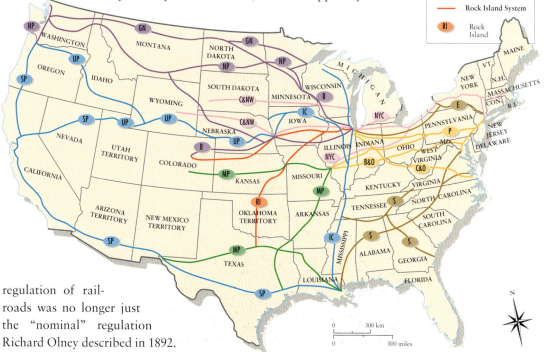

Major rail combinations, early Twentieth Century

——		Vanderbilt Roads
NYC		New York Central
C&NW		Chicago & North Western
——		Morgan Roads
S		Southern
E		Erie
——		Pennsylvania Group
P		Pennsylvania
B&O		Baltimore & Ohio
C&O		Chesapeake & Ohio
——		Harriman Roads
UP		Union Pacific
SP		Southern Pacific
IC		Illinois Central
——		Hill Roads
GN		Great Northern
NP		Northern Pacific
B		Burlington
——		Gould System
MP		Missouri Pacific
——		Rock Island System
RI		Rock Island

1916: A Record Year

The year 1916 was a year of records. In 1916 the American rail network reached an all-time high of 254,037 miles. In each year since 1830 there had been an increase in rail mileage, often thousands of miles. Between 1915 and 1916 the increase was only 248 miles, the smallest in many years. The mileage dropped over 400 miles during 1916, a decline that would continue for the rest of the 20th century. In 1916 Congress established the first federal highway program with legislation that matched state money with federal dollars for new federal highways. By 1917 nearly 5 million automobiles were registered in the nation.

The years that saw American railways reaching maturity also saw the passing of several of the great railroad builders. The hard-working and thrifty Connecticut Yankee Collis P. Huntington died in 1900, leaving behind his small cramped office in New York City. Edward H. Harriman died in 1909, and J. P. Morgan in 1913. James Jerome Hill, the "Empire Builder" in the Pacific Northwest, was buried in 1916. In that record mileage year the railways of the United States carried 98 percent of the intercity passenger business and 77 percent of the intercity freight traffic. The year 1916 probably also saw the end of the golden age of American railroading.

World War I started in Europe in August 1914. Increasing traffic soon appeared on most railroads in the country even though they were in a neutral nation thousands of miles distant from the muddy trenches of France. Most of America's railroads were not well prepared for the boom in traffic. In the fifteen years since 1900 the general price level had climbed nearly 30 percent. Railroad operating expenses rose quickly because wages, fuel, and taxes climbed even faster than the general inflation.

During the decade and a half railroad freight rates remained at 0.73¢ a ton-mile. The railroad industry's efforts to get a rate hike were unsuccessful. Public ill will had been growing for decades, and neither the general public nor the ICC was inclined to give the railroads much help in the early twentieth century. Railroad requests in 1910 for a major hike in freight rates were denied by the ICC, but a modest 5 percent increase was finally allowed. By 1914 the New

Haven, the Rock Island, the Frisco, and the Wabash were all facing bankruptcy. In 1915 more than 40,000 miles of road, a sixth of the national total, were in default or receivership.

In 1916 the four operating brotherhoods—engineers, conductors, firemen, and trainmen—demanded an eight-hour day to replace the ten-hour day in effect. President Wilson failed in his efforts at mediation. A strike was averted in September 1916 with the passage of the Adamson Act, which met most of the union demands. The railroads refused to comply and sued in the courts. A second strike was avoided when the U.S. Supreme Court, on March 19, 1917, decided in favor of the railroad unions. Two days later President Wilson issued a call for a special session of Congress that would declare war on Germany.

With the United States at war Daniel Willard, president of the B & O, and member of the Advisory Commission of the Council of National Defense, led an industry-wide effort to aid the war effort by running the nation's railroads as "a continental railway

Railroads, 1916:
254,037 miles

system." This plan was legally impossible, since it violated the 1890 Anti-Trust Act. The federal government worked out a system of priority orders for vital freight shipments, and then started to issue far too many high-priority tags. The problem was much increased by the fact that nearly all war freight shipments went in one direction—east,—to coastal shipping ports.

Soon railroad freight shipments jammed all eastern ports. The problem, of course, was made worse by the successful German submarine campaign. In a short time thousands of freight cars in eastern railroad yards were being used for storage. America's war leaders had forgotten a cardinal rule followed by General Sherman during the Civil War campaign against Atlanta: "Never use freight cars for storage."

By November 1917, the shortage of freight cars had risen to 158,000 cars. The problem was compounded by the fact that the winter of 1917 to 1918 was an early and very severe winter, which resulted in a great drop in railroad operating efficiency. On December 26, 1917, President Wilson issued a proclamation providing for federal operation of all the railroads of the nation as of December 28, 1917. William G. McAdoo, already secretary of the treasury, was made director general of the railroads.

Crowded railroad yard in 1917 during World War I. Such congestion in the East hastened federal operation of the railways.

With a large staff of railroad men McAdoo began to run the 254,000-mile rail network as a single railroad. Many changes were made. Duplicate-route passen-

American railroads in their golden age				
Year	1880	1890	1900	1916
Mileage (thousands)	93	164	193	254
Total investment ($billions)	5	9	11	21
Operating revenues ($millions)	614	1,006	1,372	3,353
Railroad employees (thousands)	419	749	1,018	1,701
Average annual wages (current $)	465	572	567	886
(1880 $)	465	602	591	620
Annual freight ton-mileage per employee (thousands)	88	101	138	215

ger trains were eliminated, sleeping-car service was curtailed, and some lightly used trains were given up. Freight shipments were permitted only if prompt delivery seemed probable. Rolling stock and engine repairs were centralized. During the months of federal control, over 1,900 locomotives and 100,000 new freight cars were constructed. The aim was not profit but an early winning of the war. During 1918 only 2 percent more freight (in ton-miles) was moved than in 1917, but the general feeling of crisis and confusion was much reduced.

Since inflation continued during the war, McAdoo decided to raise railroad wages on a sliding scale. Workers making up to $85 a month obtained a 40 percent boost, the $100-a-month man had his wage go up 31 percent, the $150-a-month wage earner received a 16 percent increase, and the $250-a-month worker had no increase at all. Wage increases continued during the war. The yearly averages were $1,003 in 1917; $1,419 in 1918; $1,485 in 1919; and $1,820 in 1920. McAdoo was forced to increase both freight rates and passenger fares during the war. In 1919 new work rules were established defining a day's work for both freight and passenger train crews. For freight train crews 100 miles of movement was a day's work; it was 150 miles for passenger train crews. Such limits were reasonable in 1918 but would later lead to featherbedding abuses.

Federal operation of the nation's railroads ended on March 1, 1920, and the Transportation Act of 1920 provided for an orderly return to private operation of the lines. The rent received by the railroads during federal control was an average of the net operating income for the three years between June 30, 1914, and June 10, 1917. Most owners would have preferred a rental based on the 1916 to 1917 year, since the 1914 to 1915 year was a year of lean profits. The ICC did raise freight rates by 25 percent for the South and the West, and by 40 percent for the East. The owners were happy to get their lines back in 1920, since in 1919 there had been some discussion of having the government purchase all the railroads for federal operation. In 1920 the owners were determined that in the event of another war they would provide a wholehearted cooperative war effort to avoid another period of federal operation.

Competition for the Railroad

Common types of steam locomotives (1848–1936). The Whyte System of locomotive type classifies engines by wheel arrangement, from front to rear. Thus the American type is ooOO while the Prairie is oOOOo.

The steam engine was perfected in the late eighteenth century, and half a century later the steam-powered railroad appeared and helped industrialize the Western world. The internal-combustion engine was perfected in the late nineteenth century, and within a short half century the automobile, the bus, the truck, and the airlines had all appeared and were increasingly competing with the railroad. Some friends of the railroad, at least in hindsight, were inclined to believe that the railroad regulation of the Progressive Era might have been unneeded—that the fruits of the internal-combustion engine would have themselves easily tamed the iron horse.

During 1895 only four automobiles were built in the United States. In 1907 the president of Princeton University, Woodrow Wilson, told his students, "Nothing has spread socialistic feelings in this country more than the automobile. . . ." Nobody could claim that the 15 million black and ungainly Model T Fords built between 1908 and 1927 helped bring socialism to America. In 1925 the price of a Model T roadster was only $260. Motor vehicle registrations in the United States climbed from 3 million in 1916, to 9 million in 1921, and to 23 million in 1929. Many American families purchased their first automobile during the 1920s. State and federal gasoline taxes, first introduced in Oregon in 1919, paid for much of the new and improved highways in the mid-twentieth century, but 40 percent of the cost came from public tax money. The number of railroad passengers dropped from 1 billion in 1916 to 700 million in 1930, and to 450 million in 1940. Railroad passenger-miles in 1929 were 34 billion, but private automobile passenger-miles were five times greater, or 175 billion.

Intercity buses and trucks also challenged the railroads, but the bus competition was the first to have a serious effect. In 1929 bus traffic made up 15 percent of all intercity commercial passenger traffic, while truck traffic made up only 3 percent of all commercial intercity freight traffic. By 1950 bus traffic had climbed to 38 percent, while truck traffic was only up to 16 percent.

By the late 1930s the dependable DC-3 airliner was proving very successful, but in 1939 airline passenger traffic was only 2 percent of all commercial passenger traffic. After World War II airline traffic quickly expanded. Railroads, buses, and airliners were nearly equal in passenger miles by 1956—railroads, 34.8 percent; buses, 31 percent; and airliners, 31.5 percent. Of course in a few more years the jet liners were clearly out in front, with buses and Amtrak far behind.

Highway truck traffic was much more enduring than highway bus traffic. The 3 million miles of highways and roads in the nation gave the truck greater convenience and flexibility than the railroad. Less-than-car-load lot freight was quickly lost by the railroads, dropping from 51 million tons in 1919 to only 1 million tons in 1966. The movement of household furniture was soon taken over by the highway moving van. The number of railroad livestock cars declined as farm and commercial trucks started moving farm hogs and cattle to packing plants. Many factory products began to be delivered by highway truck. Much of the new truck freight had been high rate shipments for the railroads; so railroad dollar losses were greater than tonnage losses.

One final type of competition in the twentieth century, the electric interurban, did not last very long. Between 1901 and 1908 over 9,000 miles of interurban routes were built in the nation, and they reached a peak of over 15,000 miles by 1916. Two-thirds of the mileage was in Illinois, Indiana, Ohio, Michigan, Pennsylvania, and New York. Intercity buses and the private automobile were too much for the interurban, and only 3,000 miles were still in service by 1941, the year of Pearl Harbor.

Federal highway system, 1925

Streamliners in the 1930s

The new competition after World War I was especially hard on railroad passenger traffic, not only in volume, but also in profits. The railroad industry has shown annual deficits for their passenger service every year since 1929, except for the four war years of 1942 through 1945. This decline in passenger traffic hit all the railroads. On the Burlington the number of passengers carried dropped from 18 million in 1924, to 14 million in 1929, and to 7 million in 1933. Burlington passenger revenue slid from $28.5 million in 1923 to $6.7 million in 1933.

Ralph Budd, the new Burlington president in 1932, had in mind a new lightweight train for local service that would be inexpensive to operate. He ordered a three-car train from the Edward G. Budd Company of Philadelphia, to be powered by a two-cycle diesel engine designed by Charles F. Kettering of General Motors. The stainless steel streamline *Zephyr* (named for the Greek god of the west wind) had a length of 196 feet, a weight of only 97 tons, and cost $200,000 to build. The new train could carry 72 passengers plus baggage and express. After the *Zephyr* had completed a shakedown tour of the East in the spring of 1934, President Budd announced that the streamliner would attempt a nonstop dawn-to-dusk run of 15 hours from Denver to Chicago to help reopen the Century of Progress Fair on May 26, 1934.

The *Zephyr* left Denver at 5:05 A.M. on May 26th with three dozen Burlington officers and several reporters on board. For the first hour or so the

The pioneer Zephyr *nears Chicago on May 16, 1934, as it completes a 785-minute nonstop trip from Denver to Chicago, a distance of 1,015 miles.*

C O L O R A

Denver
5:05 A.M.

train's speed was held down, but at the Nebraska border the speed was above 100 miles per hour. To test the smoothness of the ride Ralph Budd shaved himself with a straight-edge razor. Later in the morning a steel door accidentally cut a cable. Repairs were made as Roy Baer, a mechanic, burned his hands holding two cable ends together. The speeding train reached Lincoln, Nebraska, at 12:12 P.M.; Burlington, Iowa, at

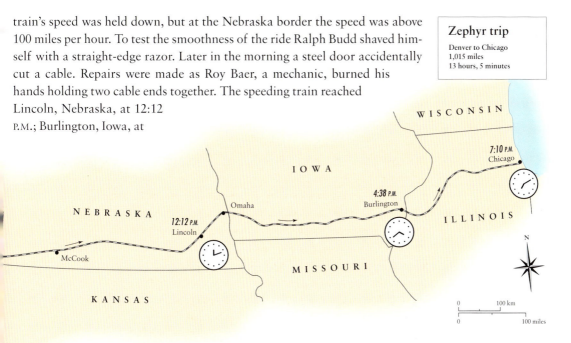

Zephyr trip

Denver to Chicago
1,015 miles
13 hours, 5 minutes

4:38 P.M.; and Halmsted Street, Chicago, at 7:10 P.M. This 1015 mile run was made in 13 hours and 5 minutes with an average speed of 77.6 miles per hour. The diesel motor had used 418 gallons of fuel oil (2.8 miles per gallon) at a total fuel cost of $14.64! After spending the summer at the Chicago World's Fair the *Zephyr* was later given a daily 500-mile round-trip run between Lincoln, Omaha, and Chicago.

Other railroads quickly noted the success of the new Burlington streamliner. The Union Pacific, which had been using several McKeen Motor Cars on branch lines for many years, built the *M-10000* in 1934 as an answer to the *Zephyr*. The $200,000 *M-10000*, a three-car aluminum alloy streamliner, weighed 85 tons and had a capacity of 116 passengers. Later renamed the *City of Salina*, the new train was placed in daily operation between Kansas City and Salina, Kansas. In 1936 the Santa Fe introduced the diesel-powered streamliner the *Super Chief* for a 39-hour run from Chicago to Los Angeles. In the same year the Illinois Central's *Green Diamond*, a diesel streamliner, gave passenger service from Chicago to St. Louis. Neither the *Super Chief* nor the *Green Diamond* was a lightweight passenger train.

These popular new diesel streamliner passenger trains slowed the decline in rail passenger traffic in the mid-1930s and also improved the quality of the service. In the 1940s and 1950s diesel motive power steadily replaced steam motive power for freight operations. Diesel locomotives had an original cost several times that of the replaced steam engines. But in hours of service, consumption of fuel, and costs of maintenance diesel motive power provided immense economic advantages.

Another War Won

Increase in operating efficiency, railroad freight service			
Year	1921	1940	change (in %)
Average freight car capacity, in tons	42.5	50.0	+ 17
Daily mileage per serviceable freight car	25.8	38.7	+ 50
Daily ton-mileage per serviceable freight car, in ton-miles	448	661	+ 48
Average length of freight train, in cars	37.4	49.7	+ 33
Average net tonnage carried by freight train, in tons	651	849	+ 30
Average freight train speed (including all stops), in m.p.h	11.5	16.7	+ 45
Net ton-mileage per freight train hour, in ton-miles	7,506	14,027	+ 87
Annual ton-mileage per freight service per railroad employee, in ton-miles	181,000	358,000	+ 98
Coal required to move 1,000 gross tons one mile, in pounds	162	112	− 31
Payments for loss and damage of freight per revenue car loaded, in $	235	55	− 77

In 1945 the railway mileage in the nation had been in decline for three decades—254,037 miles in 1916, the record high; 249,052 in 1930; and 226,696 in 1945. The decline had been only 5,000 miles from 1916 to 1930, the years of World War I and the prosperous 1920s. During the depression 1930s and World War II the mileage drop had been over 12,000 miles. In 1945 Texas, with 15,696 miles, was in first place in total mileage, a spot it had held since 1910. Following Texas were the states of Illinois, Pennsylvania, Iowa and Kansas.

Many railroads had been in serious financial trouble during the Depression. The industry had suffered deficits in net income for the years 1932, 1933, 1934, and 1938. For the decade the average rate of return for the industry was only 2.25 percent. Even so, great increases in operating efficiency had been achieved since 1920.

As the country faced a world war for the second time in a generation, the nation's railroads made every effort to escape the federal control they had known from 1917 to 1920. Even before Pearl Harbor the national-defense program and the Lend-Lease Act brought a measure of prosperity to the railroads after the long depression. The year 1940 produced a greater operating revenue than any year since 1930. In May 1940 President Franklin D. Roosevelt appointed Ralph Budd to be transportation commissioner of the Advisory Commission to the Council of National Defense. After Pearl Harbor, Roosevelt appointed Joseph B. Eastman, a longtime ICC member, to be director of the Office of Defense Transportation. Eastman found the entire rail industry very anxious to substitute full cooperation for federal control. The only period of federal control of the railroads was during a short period of labor trouble in December 1943 and January 1944.

One advantage that World War II had over World War I was that it was a two-front war with both coasts busy with war shipments to either Europe or the far Pacific. With better planning the large shortages of freight cars typical

Female workers for the B&O in World War II at Camden Station in Baltimore.

of 1917 and 1918 were avoided in the early 1940s. Each of the years in World War II saw much larger troop and war materiel shipments than were present in 1917 and 1918. The heavy increase in war traffic brought thousands of retired rail workers back to work, plus other thousands of women and high school students

into the railroad work. The heavy wartime traffic lowered the operating ratio to a low 67.5 percent for the years 1941 to 1945. Railroad profits were up and the nation's railways were able to repay $2 billion of their funded debt. During World War I the federal operation of railroads had cost taxpayers $2 million every day. During World War II the nation's rail lines paid an average of $3 million in income taxes to Uncle Sam each day of the war.

U.S. Army tanks on a New York Central freight train going to embarkation ports in World War II.

During the early 1940s the several land-grant lines had given the federal government huge discounts on all the government wartime traffic. In 1946 the federal government estimated that total land-grant discounts for the century since 1850 amounted to about $900 million, or an average of $6 or $7 for each of the 131 million acres given as land grants. Congress passed legislation in 1946 ending all discounts by land grant lines for federal government traffic.

Railroads, 1945:
226,696 miles

American Railroads in 1950

World War II had brought a relative prosperity to the railroads of the United States. Railroad operating revenues in 1943, 1944, and 1945 were more than twice those in the early 1930s. The yearly railway revenues of the late 1940s declined only moderately from those of the war years. Total rail mileage had dropped more than 15,000 miles in the depression 1930s, but only 10,000 miles during the 1940s, standing at 223,779 miles in 1950. The operating ratio (the ratio of operating expenses to operating revenue) for the industry had climbed after the end of the war, averaging 78.6 percent for the years 1946 to 1950. For the year 1950 the operating ratio was down to 74.5 percent. Since World War II eastern lines have normally had operating ratios two or three points higher than western roads.

Total operating revenue for the entire industry in 1950 was $9.47 billion, and operating expenses were $7.05 billion. In 1950 passenger revenue was about 10 percent of the freight revenue. In the 1920s passenger revenue had been about 20 percent of the freight figure. In 1950 the average yearly revenue across the nation was about $42,000 for each mile of railroad line. Trunk area lines and "coal roads" tended to be well above that average. Southern and transcontinental railroads tended to be near the average, while midwestern lines were often below the average. Railroad employment in 1950 for the entire industry was 1,220,784, or about 5.5 workers per mile of road. Employment in 1950 was about 20 percent above the depression 1930s and 15 percent below that of World War II. The average annual wage for railroad workers in 1950 was $3,763. (Railroads normally spend about half of their revenue on wages.)

The following several chapters will review the history of and provide the 1950 statistics for twenty-six important American railroads. Together the twenty-six represent 81 percent of the industry's total revenue, 77 percent of the mileage, and 74 percent of the workforce. The lines will be presented in five groups: four trunk area lines; seven southern roads; five transcontinental roads; four Granger lines; and six eastern, midwestern, and southwestern railroads.

Right:
The old and the new. The 1864 C. P. Huntington alongside a giant Southern Pacific diesel.

Far right:
A B&O chef keeps busy in his efficient and well-planned galley.

Baltimore & Ohio Railroad

1950 Statistics	
(Moody's Railroads, 1951)	
Mileage	6,187
Number of states served	13
Freight revenue (millions)	$353
Passenger revenue (millions)	$22
Passenger revenue as % of freight revenue	6%
Total revenue (millions)	$403
Net income (millions)	$15
Operating ratio	80.6%
Employees	53,592
Workers per mile of line	8.6
Revenue per mile of line	$67,000
Locomotives	1,911
% diesel	22%
Freight cars	89,309
Passenger cars	1,315

The Baltimore & Ohio Railroad was granted a charter in 1827 and was the first railway projected over the Allegheny Mountains to the Ohio Valley. As one of America's early railroads, the journalist Lucius Beebe once called the B&O the "Mother of Railroads." The line was the answer of the city of Baltimore to New York City's successful Erie Canal, as the merchants of Baltimore sought to capture the trade of the West. The B&O reached the upper Ohio River in 1852, and by 1860 the 515-mile line had revenue of $4 million. During the Civil War the B&O was the most vulnerable to Confederate attack of the several trunk lines serving the mid-Atlantic states. John W. Garrett, a Baltimore commission merchant, was president of the line from 1856 to 1884. He pushed his

Daniel Willard. The fourteenth president of the Baltimore & Ohio (1910–41) was a popular leader.

line to Chicago in 1874 and soon was engaged in rate wars with both the Pennsylvania and New York Central roads. The B&O played a major role in starting the serious railroad strike of 1877. By 1884 the B&O was a system of 1,700 miles and had a workforce of 20,000 men and an annual revenue of $19 million.

During the late 1890s the B&O was in receivership but was successfully reorganized in 1899. Early in the next century the B&O was under the control of the Pennsylvania Railroad but was independent again by 1908. Daniel Willard became president of the road in 1910, retaining that position until 1941. He was by far the most popular president in the history of the railroad. In 1910 the B&O was a system of 4,400 miles, with a workforce of over 50,000, and a yearly revenue of $80 million. Willard greatly expanded the mileage and upgraded both the motive power and the rolling stock. With the Fair of the Iron Horse held near Baltimore in 1927 he honored the centennial of the railroad. The B&O suffered large declines in revenue during the depression 1930s but managed to escape receivership. The B&O did not resume dividends until 1953.

The B&O was a major trunk line but clearly ranked well below the Pennsylvania Railroad and the New York Central both in freight and passenger service. It had an excellent reputation for its safe and comfortable

passenger service and was an early leader in air-conditioned passenger service. Since the B&O had a fairly large traffic in soft coal, it was not as rapid as many other lines to shift from steam to diesel motive power. In the late 1950s the B&O had major declines in operating revenue, and in 1962 it was acquired by the far more prosperous Chesapeake & Ohio Railway. Since then it has become a major part of both the Chessie system and, its successor, the CSX.

Pennsylvania Railroad

1950 Statistics	
(Moody's Railroads, 1951)	
Mileage	10,184
Number of states served	13
Freight revenue (millions)	$686
Passenger revenue (millions)	$142
Passenger revenue as % of freight revenue	21%
Total revenue (millions)	$930
Net income (millions)	$38
Operating ratio	84.3%
Employees	124,629
Workers per mile of line	12.2
Revenue per mile of line	$93,000
Locomotives	3,800
% diesel	30%
Freight cars	191,490
Passenger cars	4,954

Although the Pennsylvania Railroad in 1950 led the country in freight revenue, passenger revenue, and size of workforce, it was the last of the four trunk lines to be organized. In the spring of 1846 a number of Philadelphia merchants received a charter from the state to build a 248-mile railroad from Harrisburg to Pittsburgh. The passage of the charter legislation was a defeat for the Baltimore & Ohio, which had been eager to build a branch from western Maryland north to Pittsburgh. Later the new Pennsylvania Railroad acquired from the state certain short railways and inclined planes that were part of the unsuccessful Pennsylvania Main Line.

John Edgar Thompson, who had earlier helped build the Georgia Railroad, was at once named chief engineer to survey and build the projected railroad to Pittsburgh. By 1855 the 355-mile line from Philadelphia to Pittsburgh was finished. Thompson was president of the Pennsylvania from 1852 until his death in 1874. By that year the Pennsylvania controlled a 1,599-mile network extending from New York City, Philadelphia, and Washington, D.C., to Chicago and St. Louis with yearly revenue of $37 million. Thomson ran his railroad as an efficient business and did much to earn for his line the reputation for being the "Standard" railroad of the country.

In 1899, when Alexander J. Cassatt became the road's president, the Pennsylvania was a 2,850-mile railroad with yearly revenue of $73 million and

Thomas A. Scott. Similar to Jay Gould, Scott had interests in many railroads, but his main concern was with the Pennsylvania.

a net income of $11 million. When Cassatt died in office in 1906 the line was up to 4,000 miles, the revenue had doubled, and the net income had nearly tripled. Cassatt directed the planning and building of the tunnels under the Hudson River (opened in 1907) and of the Pennsylvania Station in New York City (opened in 1910). New electric locomotives were needed for the new tubes under the Hudson.

By 1925 the Pennsylvania was a system of 10,600 miles with a revenue of $672 million and a net income of $69 million. In the early 1920s passenger revenue was about 30 percent of freight revenue. The Pennsylvania extended its electrified mileage to Washington, D.C., in 1931, and later to Harrisburg. By midcentury 664 miles had been electrified. Improved electric motive power was built in the 1930s, and in 1935 the powerful streamlined class GG1 was added to the electric motive power roster. Eventually 139 GG1 locomotives were in use.

Pennsylvania common stock was widely held—by World War II 200,000 people held the stock of the "Standard" railroad. One reason was that the railroad had paid dividends (cash or stock) every year since 1856. But competitive

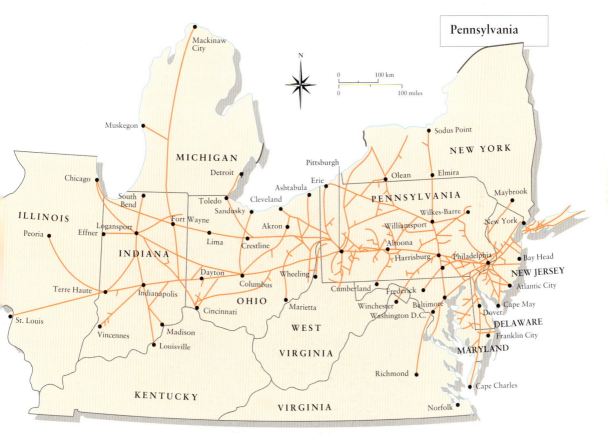

modes of transport, the decline of heavy industry in the northeast, and aging equipment were all taking their toll in the post-war years. Total ton-mileage dropped by a third between the late 1940s and 1960. The lure of mergers brought the Penn Central marriage of 1968 and the staggering bankruptcy of 1970.

New York Central Railroad

1950 Statistics	
(Moody's Railroads, 1951)	
Mileage	10,727
Number of states served	11
Freight revenue (millions)	$545
Passenger revenue (millions)	$117
Passenger revenue as % of freight revenue	21%
Total revenue (millions)	$760
Net income (millions)	$18
Operating ratio	83.3%
Employees	110,950
Workers per mile of line	9.5
Revenue per mile of line	$69,000
Locomotives	3,489
% diesel	34%
Freight cars	143,761
Passenger cars	4,972

The New York Central, unlike the other three major trunk lines, was not the result of building a long-planned route, but was rather a system achieved by acquiring or leasing smaller roads already in operation. The first New York Central was a 298-mile line running from Albany to Buffalo. It was created in 1853 out of ten short lines strung like beads on a string parallel to the Mohawk Valley and the Erie Canal. Prime mover in the consolidation was Erastus Corning, iron manufacturer of Albany and longtime president of the 78-mile Utica & Schenectady. Corning had never had a salary as president, being content to sell the U&S all its rail and iron needs. This cozy arrangement was not long tolerated by the larger New York Central. We noted earlier how Vanderbilt, in the icy winter of 1867, took over the New York Central. In 1869 the Commodore consolidated the New York Central, the New York & Harlem, and the New York & Hudson into a new New York Central & Hudson River Railroad.

Vanderbilt ran his enlarged system with style. He banned both color and brass on his well-built locomotives, which were called "Black Crooks" by their engine crews. Vanderbilt voted himself a $6 million bonus and inflated the capital structure of the rail system with at least $20 million of new watered stock.

Commodore Cornelius Vanderbilt. Vanderbilt's first interest in railroading came in 1862, when he was 68 and already a millionaire.

But the New York Central & Hudson River was very efficiently operated. Even during the depression 1870s, annual dividends of 6 to 8 percent were paid on the inflated capital structure.

Before the Commodore died in 1877 his line had taken over two lines to Chicago—the Lake Shore & Michigan Southern (south of Lake Erie), and the Michigan Central (north of Lake Erie). In 1877 the Commodore's eldest son, William H. Vanderbuilt, inherited the entire rail system, which was valued at $90 million. When William died in 1884 the railroad was worth $200 million. In the mid-1880s the Central had acquired the Cleveland, Cincinnati, St. Louis & Chicago, a 2,000-mile road in Ohio, Indiana, and Illinois. By 1900 the Boston & Albany had also been leased. In 1900 these five Vanderbilt lines had a combined 8,500 miles of road, revenue of $86 million, and an average operating ratio of 64 percent.

A century ago a definite rivalry existed between the New York Central and the Pennsylvania. The Central's *No. 999*, a high-wheeled 4-4-0 reached a speed of 112.5 miles an hour in 1893, but a Pennsylvania engine had 127 miles per hour in 1905. In 1913 the Grand Central Terminal was opened in midtown Manhattan to match the earlier Pennsylvania Station. In 1914 the words "and Hudson River R.R." were deleted from the title, leaving "New York Central R.R." In 1902 the Central's *Twentieth Century* and the *Broadway* were both introduced for the deluxe all-Pullman passenger trade. After World War II the Central faced the same troubles as the Pennsylvania—higher wages and taxes, and increased truck traffic—making it hard to make a profit and pay dividends. The Penn Central merger was cut short by the 1970 bankruptcy.

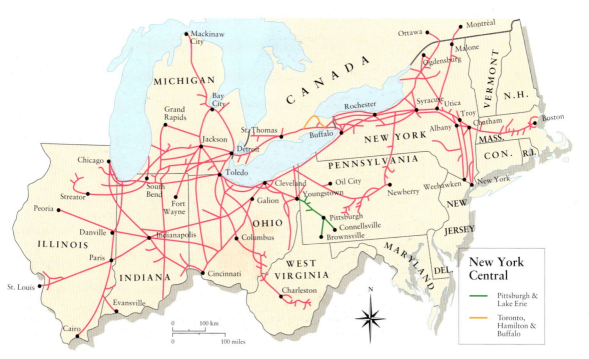

New York Central

— Pittsburgh & Lake Erie

— Toronto, Hamilton & Buffalo

Erie Railroad

1950 Statistics	
(Moody's Railroads, 1951)	
Mileage	2,022
Number of states served	6
Freight revenue (millions)	$147
Passenger revenue (millions)	$7
Passenger revenue as % of freight revenue	5%
Total revenue (millions)	$166
Net income (millions)	$13
Operating ratio	73.2%
Employees	21,456
Workers per mile of line	10.6
Revenue per mile of line	$83,000
Locomotives	485
% diesel	52%
Freight cars	24,504
Passenger cars	662

An Erie Railway ad in the years when Jay Gould and Commodore Vanderbilt were fighting to control Erie.

The New York & Erie Railway, generally known as the Erie, was granted a state charter in 1832 to build a line through the southern tier of counties in New York from Piermont-on-Hudson (25 miles north of New York City) to Dunkirk on Lake Erie. Eleazor Lord, first president of the Erie, had two unique ideas—build the railroad in the broad six-foot gauge and use pilings instead of the normal roadbed. Pilings were soon abandoned, and the offbeat broad gauge lasted only until 1878. In 1845, when Benjamin Loder replaced Lord as president, only 53 miles of the Erie line was complete. Loder, a hard-headed New York City dry goods merchant, found new money and completed the 460-mile road in 1851 at the cost of $23 million. At midcentury the Erie had several inherent weaknesses—both of its terminals were only hamlets, there were no cities of any size along its route, and it was difficult to reach either Buffalo or New York City.

In 1851 the Erie was reported to be the longest railroad in the world. It celebrated its completion with a grand celebration in mid-May with two passenger trains headed for Dunkirk. On board were many dignitaries, including President Millard Fillmore and several of his cabinet members. Daniel Webster sat in a rocking chair fastened to a flat car, bundled up in a steamer rug with a flask of Medford rum for company. Fifteen years later bankruptcy brought the line a new name, Erie Railway, with Daniel Drew, Jay Gould, and Jim Fisk in control. Finding that Cornelius Vanderbilt wished to buy into Erie, Jay Gould sold the Commodore 150,000 shares of worthless stock. After his experience with "the Scarlet Woman" of Wall Street, Vanderbilt grumbled, "It learned me never to kick a skunk."

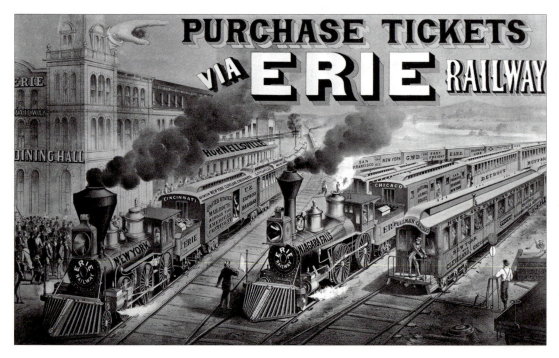

The Erie was reorganized again in 1874 as the New York, Lake Erie and Western Railroad. With a leased line to the west the road had a 998-mile main line from Jersey City, New Jersey, west to Chicago. In 1900 the Erie was a 2,271-mile railroad with revenue of $39 million, an operating ratio of 72 percent, and a debt of $238 million. From 1901 to 1926 Frederick Underwood was president of the Erie. Underwood made many improvements on his railroad, including double-tracking some of the main line and adding new bridges, block signals, and larger locomotives. During the Underwood years the Erie earned its nickname, "Old Reliable."

The depression of the 1930s found the Erie again in receivership in 1938. The wartime traffic after 1940 permitted a real rarity on the Erie, a 1942 dividend on the common stock. Traffic slowed in the postwar years, and in the early 1960s the Erie found a merger companion in the Delaware, Lackawanna & Western. The Erie–Lackawanna itself was in receivership in 1972 and became a part of Conrail in 1976.

Erie Railroad agents were the first to use telegraph for the dispatching of trains—on September 22, 1851.

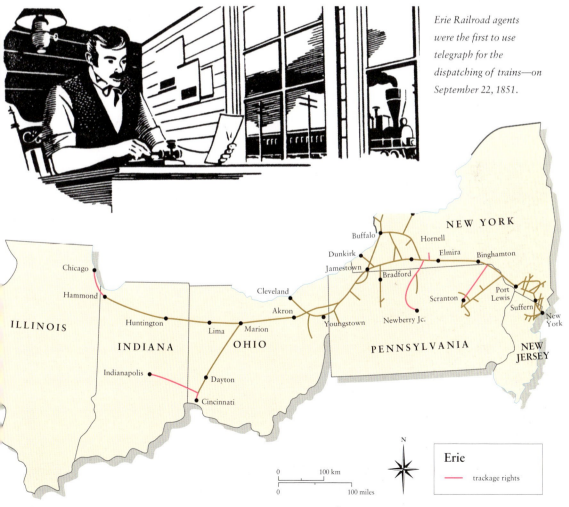

Southern Railway

1950 Statistics	
(Moody's Railroads, 1951)	
Mileage	6,367
Number of states served	11
Freight revenue (millions)	$202
Passenger revenue (millions)	$16
Passenger revenue as % of freight revenue	8%
Total revenue (millions)	$240
Net income (millions)	$22
Operating ratio	70.2%
Employees	32,050
Workers per mile of line	5.0
Revenue per mile of line	$40,000
Locomotives	1,142
% diesel	38%
Freight cars	37,980
Passenger cars	930

The Charleston & Hamburg, one of the dozens of short southern lines that would ultimately be merged to form the Southern Railway, made its first scheduled run in 1830. A more important predecessor line was the 143-mile Richmond & Danville, a railroad that served as a major transportation artery of the beleaguered Confederate capital during the Civil War. In 1871 Tom Scott, vice president of the Pennsylvania Railroad, purchased the state-owned common stock of the Richmond & Danville. By the mid-1870s the Pennsylvania controlled thirteen southern lines in six states, with a total of 2,100 miles. The depression in the 1870s forced the northern road to sell the bulk of its southern system, but it retained the R&D, which was sold in 1880 to the W. P. Clyde Syndicate.

The Clyde Syndicate obtained a charter from Virginia for creating the Richmond and West Point Terminal Railway & Warehouse Company, a holding company. The parent, Richmond & Danville, plus its holding company controlled a rail system amounting to 2,600 miles in 1885 and more than 5,000 miles in the early 1890s. When the R&D and the Richmond Terminal system collapsed in the early 1890s Drexel, Morgan & Company was given the task of reorganization.

In 1894 J. P. Morgan and his associates selected the thirty strongest lines from the total R&D system and merged them into the newly formed Southern

Samuel Spencer. Spencer was the first president, 1894–1906, of the newly formed Southern Railway.

Railway. Morgan selected Samuel Spencer, his bank's railroad expert, to be the president of the new 4,400-mile railway located in seven states. The mileage of the new railway grew to 6,300 miles by 1900, and the yearly revenue climbed from $16 million to $31 million in the same six years. Most of the line's net income was used for improvements in road and equipment. The Southern Railway paid no dividends on its common stock until after World War I.

The strongest presidents of the Southern Railway in the twentieth century have been Samuel Spencer (1894–1906), Fairfax Harrison (1913–37), Harry A. DeButts (1952–62), and W. Graham Claytor, Jr. (1967–76). Since World War II the Southern Railway, the longest line in the South, has been noted for its modernization and innovation, including early dieselization,

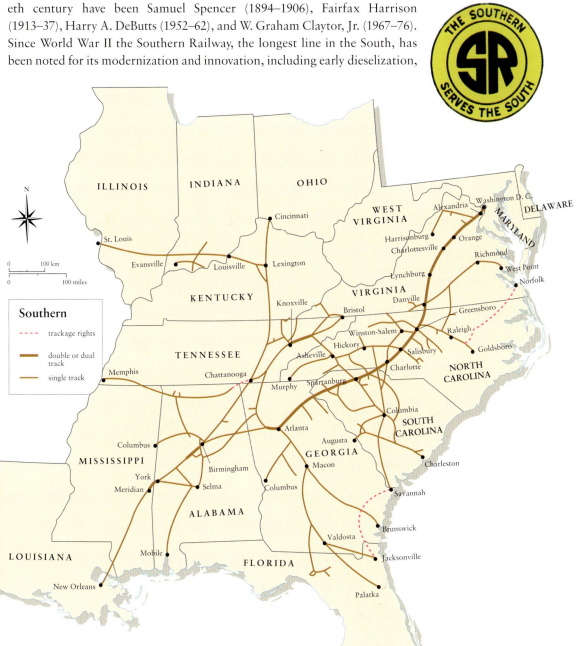

mechanization of track maintenance, the extensive use of computers and microwave communication, improved car usage, and a tight fiscal policy. In 1974 *Dun's Review* listed the Southern Railway as among the five "Best-Managed Companies" in the nation. When the Southern Railway in 1982 merged with the Norfolk & Western to form the 17,000-mile Norfolk Southern, it represented the joining of two of the most prosperous roads in America.

Louisville & Nashville Railroad

1950 Statistics

(Moody's Railroads, 1951)

Mileage	4,778
Number of states served	13
Freight revenue (millions)	$176
Passenger revenue (millions)	$13
Passenger revenue as % of freight revenue	7%
Total revenue (millions)	$203
Net income (millions)	$26
Operating ratio	74.2%
Employees	27,150
Workers per mile of line	5.6
Revenue per mile of line	$42,000
Locomotives	842
% diesel	24%
Freight cars	60,327
Passenger cars	634

Early in 1850 the states of Kentucky and Tennessee chartered the Louisville & Nashville Railroad, with the city of Louisville subscribing to bonds and Tennessee offering $10,000 per mile of track. By 1856 only 30 miles of line were in operation. It remained for one of the first citizens of Louisville—the lame, uncouth, but highly regarded James Guthrie—to push the L&N project with new vigor upon his return from Pierce's cabinet late in 1857. With help from Albert Fink the L&N was completed to Nashville late in 1859. A branch line to Memphis gave the L&N 253 miles in operation by 1860. The railroad suffered only minor damage from the Civil War and was paying high dividends in the postwar years. The road was expanded in the 1870s and had nearly 1,000 miles in operation in 1879. The L&N soon had effective control of the Nashville, Chattanooga & St. Louis. By the early 1880s New York City investors were in control of the L&N. In the mid-1880s the L&N extended from St. Louis and Cincinnati in the north to New Orleans and Mobile in the south.

Milton Hannibal Smith was president of the L&N from 1884 to 1886, and from 1891 to 1921, the year of his death. The gruff and cantankerous Smith viewed the entire region south of Louisville and the Ohio River as an economic wilderness created for the business of his railroad. Smith liked to have fancy brass work on his locomotives but hated passenger services, allowing most of his coaches to become antiques. He felt that profits only came from freight traffic and built new branches to any new mine or factory. Between 1884 and 1921 the L&N system increased from 2,065 to 5,041 miles, and the yearly revenue rose from $14 million to $117 million. In the same years dividends as high as 7 percent were paid in all but eight years.

The L&N was a prosperous road, was never in receivership, and was called by many patrons the "Old Reliable." It paid good dividends from 1900 to 1967, except for the two depression years of 1932 and 1933. Because of its heavy coal traffic the L&N was slow to accept diesels, but by the mid-1950s it shifted fully to the new type of motive power. The L&N system was located west of Appalachia, and its most eastern lines were in western Virginia and North Carolina, Atlanta, and the western panhandle of Florida. The new Seaboard Coast Line greatly increased its holdings of L&N stock in the late 1970s and took over the L&N in 1982. Later the L&N became a part of the CSX Corporation.

DIXIE LINE

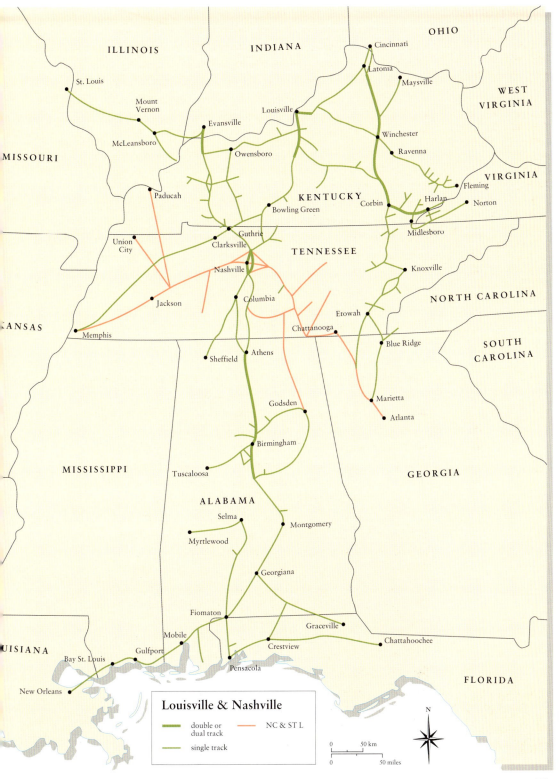

OHIO

ILLINOIS

INDIANA

Cincinnati

Latonia

Maysville

WEST
VIRGINIA

St. Louis

Mount
Vernon

Louisville

Evansville

McLeansboro

Owensboro

Winchester

Ravenna

MISSOURI

VIRGINIA

Fleming

Paducah

KENTUCKY

Bowling Green

Corbin

Harlan

Norton

Union
City

Guthrie

Clarksville

Midlesboro

TENNESSEE

Nashville

Jackson

Columbia

Knoxville

NORTH CAROLINA

Etowah

Memphis

Chattanooga

Blue Ridge

SOUTH
CAROLINA

ARKANSAS

Sheffield

Athens

Godsden

Marietta

Atlanta

Birmingham

Tuscaloosa

MISSISSIPPI

GEORGIA

ALABAMA

Selma

Montgomery

Myrtlewood

Georgiana

Fiomaton

Graceville

Mobile

Chattahoochee

Crestview

LOUISIANA

Gulfport

Bay St. Louis

Pensacola

FLORIDA

New Orleans

Louisville & Nashville

— double or
dual track

— NC & ST L

— single track

0   50 km

0   50 miles

N

Illinois Central Railroad

1950 Statistics	
(Moody's Railroads, 1951)	
Mileage	6,539
Number of states served	13
Freight revenue (millions)	$224
Passenger revenue (millions)	$22
Passenger revenue as % of freight revenue	10%
Total revenue (millions)	$276
Net income (millions)	$29
Operating ratio	72.6%
Employees	37,539
Workers per mile of line	5.8
Revenue per mile of line	$42,000
Locomotives	1,262
% diesel	11%
Freight cars	53,899
Passenger cars	1,077

While the Illinois Central has lines in all three districts—eastern, southern, and western, the ICC has assigned the road to the southern district, as a southern railroad. The Illinois Central was chartered by Illinois in 1851 after the U.S. Congress granted the proposed line a 2.5 million acre land grant in 1850. The railroad was to run north from Cairo to Dunleith, with a branch to Chicago, thus serving most of the state. Eastern investors from New York City, Boston, and Europe financed the road but construction was slow until William Osborn, a Boston merchant, became president in 1855. When the 705-mile IC was completed in 1856 it was the longest railroad in the world. The new road seemed to be running the "wrong way" since most lines built in the 1850s in the old Northwest were built east to west. During the Civil War the IC moved thousands of Union troops under General U. S. Grant south to Cairo as he started his campaign against Forts Henry and Donelson.

By 1870 the IC controlled a line across Iowa from Dubuque to Sioux City. In the 1870s the Illinois Central gained control of the Chicago, St. Louis & New Orleans, a line from Cairo to New Orleans, by ousting Colonel Henry S. McComb, a carpetbagger from Delaware. By 1883 the IC was operating 1,927 miles of line with annual revenue of $13 million. In 1901 the railroad celebrated its golden anniversary by revealing that for the first time Americans, instead of Europeans, held a majority of the common stock. Stuyvesant Fish was president of the IC, but Edward H. Harriman was in firm control of the road. At the turn of the century the IC was known as the "Main Line of Mid-America."

Between 1900 and 1930 the IC expanded from 3,845 to 6,711 miles, annual revenue climbed from $37 million to $148 million, and average dividends of over $6.50 were paid each year. The depression 1930s were difficult for the railroad, revenues dropped nearly 50 percent, and the labor force declined from 60,000 in 1929 to 25,000 in 1933. The IC escaped receivership in the decade only by

Building the Illinois Central Railroad in 1856. Painting by George I. Parish Jr.

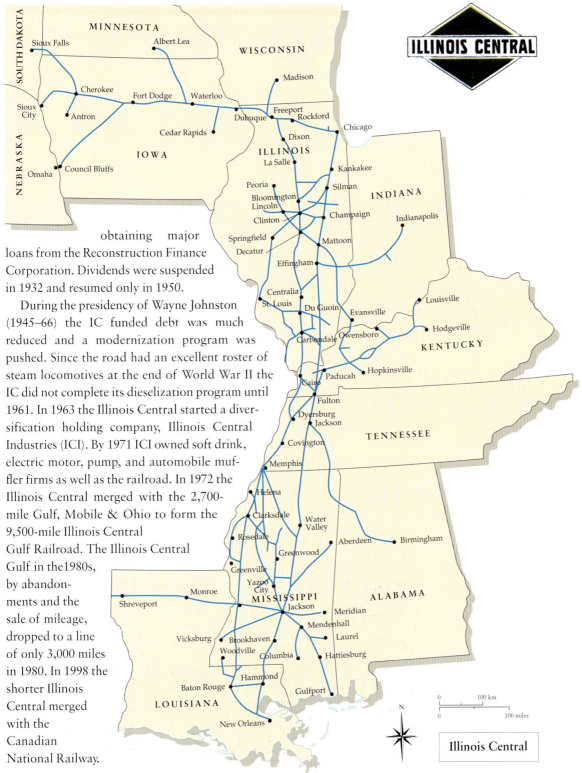

obtaining major loans from the Reconstruction Finance Corporation. Dividends were suspended in 1932 and resumed only in 1950.

During the presidency of Wayne Johnston (1945–66) the IC funded debt was much reduced and a modernization program was pushed. Since the road had an excellent roster of steam locomotives at the end of World War II the IC did not complete its dieselization program until 1961. In 1963 the Illinois Central started a diversification holding company, Illinois Central Industries (ICI). By 1971 ICI owned soft drink, electric motor, pump, and automobile muffler firms as well as the railroad. In 1972 the Illinois Central merged with the 2,700-mile Gulf, Mobile & Ohio to form the 9,500-mile Illinois Central Gulf Railroad. The Illinois Central Gulf in the1980s, by abandonments and the sale of mileage, dropped to a line of only 3,000 miles in 1980. In 1998 the shorter Illinois Central merged with the Canadian National Railway.

Atlantic Coast Line Railroad

1950 Statistics	
(*Moody's Railroads, 1951*)	
Mileage	5,452
Number of states served	6
Freight revenue (millions)	$105
Passenger revenue (millions)	$17
Passenger revenue as % of freight revenue	16%
Total revenue (millions)	$134
Net income (millions)	$13
Operating ratio	80.1%
Employees	17,127
Workers per mile of line	3.1
Revenue per mile of line	$25,000
Locomotives	758
% diesel	37%
Freight cars	27,294
Passenger cars	616

The Atlantic Coast Line, much like the Southern Railway, was a combination of many earlier lines. In 1869 William T. Walters, a Baltimore produce merchant, purchased a controlling interest in both the Wilmington & Weldon and the Wilmington & Manchester Railroads, two major lines in North and South Carolina. Later he also acquired two connecting lines between Richmond and Weldon. He was aided in these ventures by Benjamin R. Newcomer, a Baltimore banker. Known as the Weldon Route, these several lines were used to ship fresh fruit and vegetables in refrigerator cars north to Baltimore and other eastern markets. Walters and his associates created a Connecticut holding company in 1889 that organized the Atlantic Coast Line Railroad in 1893. William Walters died in 1894, and his son, Henry Walters, later was president and board chairman of the Atlantic Coast Line from 1900 until his death in 1931.

In 1900 the Atlantic Coast Line consisted of about a dozen southern roads making a system of 1,539 miles, with yearly revenue of $6 million and an operating ratio of 66 percent.

Two years later, in 1902, the Henry Bradley Plant System of 2,000 miles in Alabama, Georgia, and Florida was acquired by Henry Walters for the Atlantic Coast Line. Early in the twentieth century the Atlantic Coast Line also acquired a major share of the common stock of the Louisville & Nashville Railroad.

After the end of World War I the Atlantic Coast Line double tracked its main line from Richmond to Jacksonville and also installed automatic block signaling. Both the Atlantic Coast Line and the Seaboard Air Line had a larger passenger traffic than most other railways in the south. The Atlantic Coast Line had several fast passenger trains between New York City and Florida. Most famous was the *Florida Special,* an all Pullman train with a twenty-four-hour schedule between New York City and Florida by 1927.

After World War II the Atlantic Coast Line created an active industrial development department in order to produce new traffic for the railroad. Both the chemical and the pulp and paper industries set up new plants along the lines of the Atlantic Coast Line in North and South Carolina and Georgia. In the postwar years the shift from agricultural to industrial pursuits raised the southern urban population to 55 percent of the total population by 1960. Per capita income in the South rose more rapidly in the same years.

However, in the postwar years both highway trucks and fast air travel were becoming more competitive. By the late 1950s Atlantic Coast Line top officials were talking of a possible merger with the rival Seaboard Air Line. The Interstate Commerce Commission heard testimony on the proposal in 1961 and approved the merger, creating the new Seaboard Coast Line. Later the new company would join Chessie to form CSX.

Seaboard Air Line Railroad

1950 Statistics	
(Moody's Railroads, 1951)	
Mileage	4,146
Number of states served	6
Freight revenue (millions)	$110
Passenger revenue (millions)	$14
Passenger revenue as % of freight revenue	13%
Total revenue (millions)	$136
Net income (millions)	$14
Operating ratio	72.9%
Employees	16,636
Workers per mile of line	4.0
Revenue per mile of line	$34,000
Locomotives	628
% diesel	56%
Freight cars	21,895
Passenger cars	495

The Seaboard Air Line, like many other southern railroads, was the result of a continuing merger of many smaller lines. After the Civil War some investors from Baltimore and Philadelphia gained control of the Seaboard & Roanoke, an 80-mile line running from Portsmouth, Virginia, to Weldon, North Carolina. In the mid-1870s John M. Robinson, president of the Seaboard & Roanoke, gained control of the Raleigh & Gaston, a 97-mile road connecting Weldon and Raleigh. Later Robinson acquired three other railroads and by 1892 the expanding 800-mile rail network ran from Portsmouth down to Atlanta. Robinson's route was known as the Seaboard Air Line. The system also provided coastal steamship service from Portsmouth north to Baltimore and New York City.

In 1898 John L. Williams and Sons of Richmond and Middendorf, Oliver & Company of Baltimore, already owners of the 450-mile Georgia & Alabama, purchased the Seaboard Air Line. The new owners of the Seaboard next acquired the 940-mile Florida, Central and Peninsular Railroad, located in Florida. In 1900 the Richmond and Baltimore financiers created a new corporation for their three systems, the Seaboard Air Line Railway, formed from twenty different lines with 2,600 miles of road in six states. The new company was in receivership by 1908, being reorganized in 1909 as the Seaboard Air Line Railroad. The new company built more branch lines in Florida and shared fully in the Florida land boom of the 1920s. During that decade heavier rail was laid, double tracking added, and automatic block signaling installed. By the late twenties the SAL was a system of 4,500 miles. The crash of 1929 quickly placed the Seaboard in trouble, and the road was in bankruptcy by 1930 with a receivership that lasted until 1945.

Even though the line was in receivership, the Seaboard purchased its first diesel locomotive in 1938. The many advantages of diesel power caused the road to buy many more units, and by 1950 the line had 350 units. With 56 percent of its locomotives diesel, the Seaboard had a much larger relative diesel roster than any of the other six southern railroads. In 1950 the three major southern coal roads, the IC, C&O, and Norfolk & Western, were much slower to adopt the new form of motive power. By 1956 the Seaboard engine roster was one steamer and 500 diesel units.

World War II created a heavy traffic for the Seaboard, but the line had never developed the strong financial structure possessed by its rival, the Atlantic Coast Line. The postwar years saw a rising gross revenue, but the net income always seemed to lag behind. By the late 1950s the Seaboard was happy to consider a merger with the Atlantic Coast Line. The two joined to become the Seaboard Coast Line on July 1, 1967. This was one of the few times the Interstate Commerce Commission had approved a merger of two parallel lines unless they were in dire financial trouble. Later the Seaboard Coast Line would merge with the Louisville & Nashville, and still later with the CSX.

Chesapeake & Ohio

1950 Statistics	
(Moody's Railroads, 1951)	
Mileage	5,116
Number of states served	8
Freight revenue (millions)	$296
Passenger revenue (millions)	$8
Passenger revenue as % of freight revenue	3%
Total revenue (millions)	$319
Net income (millions)	$34
Operating ratio	69.3%
Employees	35,463
Workers per mile of line	6.9
Revenue per mile of line	$60,000
Locomotives	1,322
% diesel	20%
Freight cars	84,674
Passenger cars	545

The Chesapeake & Ohio Railway was the product of an 1868 merger of the Virginia Central Railroad and the Covington & Ohio Railroad. The president of the C&O was General William C. Wickham, a former Confederate cavalry officer. Wickham wished to extend his C&O from Covington west through West Virginia to the Ohio River. Finding no financial aid either in Virginia or in Europe, he turned to New York City and Collis P. Huntington, a Connecticut Yankee fresh from the laurels of building the Central Pacific. Huntington offered to build a 200-mile extension to the Ohio River for $15 million. Employing a workforce of 7,000 men Huntington pushed the extension to the Ohio by 1873. The cost had much exceeded the earlier contract, but vast coal fields had been discovered along the route in the mountains of West Virginia.

The 428-mile C&O was in receivership shortly after the Panic of 1873, but in the 1878 reorganization Collis Huntington continued to be president. The C&O was extended eastward to Newport News, Virginia, and westward into Ohio and Kentucky. The C&O was reorganized again in 1888 by Drexel, Morgan and Company, and a trusted Vanderbilt lieutenant, Melville E. Ingalls, was the president from 1888 to 1899. In 1900 the 1,425-mile C&O had a yearly revenue of $13 million, an operating ratio of 65 percent, and paid a 1 percent dividend.

Hays T. Watkins. In the 1970s and 1980s, Watkins created the Chessie System, and later CSX, out of several large Class I lines.

Between 1900 and 1909 the Pennsylvania Railroad held a major stock interest in the C&O. In those years the Chesapeake & Ohio gained new mileage in Ohio, Indiana, and Illinois. By 1920 the C&O was operating 2,500 miles of line in six states and had annual revenue of $90 million, with 77 percent of its freight tonnage being mine products. In the 1920s and early 1930s the Van Sweringen brothers—Otis P. and Mantis J.—were major shareholders in the C&O. In 1934 Robert R. Young, a Wall Street financier, purchased 43 percent of the Allegheny Corporation, which in turn controlled the C&O. The C&O in

1947 acquired the 1,940-mile Pere Marquette, which made the C&O a system of 5,100 miles. By the mid-twentieth century the Chesapeake & Ohio was originating more coal tonnage than any other U.S. railroad.

In 1954 Young sold his C&O securities to Cyrus S. Eaton, a Cleveland investment banker. Eaton gave Walter J. Tuohy, C&O president since 1948, a free hand concerning the future of the C&O. When officials of the New York Central suggested a merger with the C&O Tuohy pointed out that the C&O was in good financial shape while the New York Central was not. When the New York Central competed with the C&O to take over the Baltimore & Ohio, the C&O was a quick and easy winner. Later in 1968 the C&O took over the Western Maryland. In 1980 the ICC approved the merger of the Chessie System (C&O plus B&O) with the Seaboard Coast Line Industries to form the CSX Corporation. The CSX had 27,000 miles of line in twenty-two states, a roster of 70,000 employees, and yearly revenue of nearly $5 billion.

Norfolk & Western

1950 Statistics	
(Moody's Railroads, 1951)	
Mileage	2,100
Number of states served	6
Freight revenue (millions)	$155
Passenger revenue (millions)	$5
Passenger revenue as % of freight revenue	3%
Total revenue (millions)	$168
Net income (millions)	$29
Operating ratio	69.3%
Employees	21,246
Workers per mile of line	10.0
Revenue per mile of line	$80,000
Locomotives	486
% diesel	0%
Freight cars	56,943
Passenger cars	344

The Norfolk and Western Railway was a successor line of three short southern roads that merged after the Civil War. One of the three, the 80-mile Norfolk & Petersburg, was little more than a bare roadbed at war's end. General William Mahone, former president of the railroad, came home to restore it and soon was also president of the connecting South Side as well as the Virginia & Tennessee, the road to Bristol. In 1870 the three lines were merged to form the 400-mile Atlantic, Mississippi & Ohio. The rail-thin and poker-playing Mahone had a presidential salary of $25,000, equal to that of President Grant and more than twice General Beauregard's pay for managing two railroads. Critics claimed that Mahone believed that A,M&O meant "All Mine and Otelia's." (Otelia was his wife's first name.)

The Panic of 1873 forced the A,M&O into receivership in 1876, and in 1881 the banking firm of E. W. Clark and Company purchased the A,M&O to form the Norfolk & Western. Frederick J. Kimball, a partner in the Clark firm, was president of the N&W most of the period from 1883 to 1903. During those

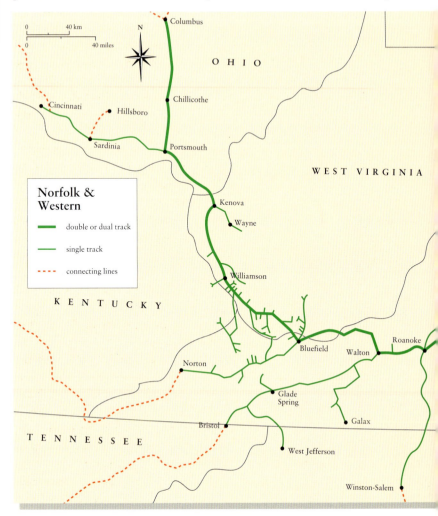

years the Norfolk & Western expanded its lines into West Virginia, North Carolina, and Ohio. When the railroad was built through the West Virginia hills, the Norfolk & Western discovered the rich bituminous outcrops that would be known as the Pocahontas Field of West Virginia. By the late 1880s the railroad was becoming a major coal road. Northern markets took a large share of the coal moved by the N&W, and the coal-loading facilities at Norfolk were much expanded to meet the needs of New York and New England. In 1887 a ton of coal at Norfolk had a price of $1.32, a figure that dropped to 80¢ by 1898. The N&W in 1900 was a 1,551 mile line with $14 million of revenue and an operating ratio of 60 percent. In 1900 coal and coke made up 60 percent of the road's freight tonnage.

Shortly after 1900 the Pennsylvania acquired a major share of the N&W capital stock, which it retained for a number of years. Coal tonnage on the N&W grew rapidly, increasing elevenfold between 1896 and 1926. The Norfolk & Western prospered and paid good dividends even during the depression 1930s. The N&W was reluctant to give up its coal-burning motive power and was one of the last of the major railroads to shift to diesels. In 1959 the Norfolk and Western acquired the Virginia Railway, a 600-mile coal road out of Norfolk with a very low grade. In 1964 the N&W merged with the Nickel Plate (New York, Chicago & St. Louis) Railroad that provided important mileage in Ohio, Indiana, and Illinois, with several ports on Lakes Michigan and Erie. By 1965 the N&W had 7,500 miles in twelve states. In 1981 the ICC approved a merger of the enlarged N&W with the Southern to form the Norfolk Southern. That new system in 1986 had a 17,000-mile network with 38,000 employees and annual revenue of $4 billion.

Union Pacific

1950 Statistics	
(Moody's Railroads, 1951)	
Mileage	9,720
Number of states served	13
Freight revenue (millions)	$389
Passenger revenue (millions)	$33
Passenger revenue as % of freight revenue	8%
Total revenue (millions)	$465
Net income (millions)	$70
Operating ratio	70.3%
Employees	52,100
Workers per mile of line	5.4
Revenue per mile of line	$47,000
Locomotives	1,539
% diesel	36%
Freight cars	49,978
Passenger cars	1,079

After the Golden Spike Celebration of 1869 the Union Pacific Railroad first had to find traffic for its line, and then face Congressional questions about the Credit Mobilier. A bit of repair or "finishing touches" also had to be made on the hastily completed road. Jay Gould gained control of the UP in 1874 and in the next few years defied his reputation by improving the service on his railroad. He also found some settlers to purchase his land-grant acres. In 1875 passenger service made up about 40 percent of the $12 million annual revenue of the line. Charles Francis Adams Jr., was president of the UP from 1884 to 1890 but had little success with either the labor or financial problems of the road.

The Panic of 1893 quickly pushed the Union Pacific into receivership. Jacob H. Schiff, of the banking firm of Kuhn, Loeb and Company, headed up the committee that was trying to reorganize the Union Pacific. In 1898 a new Union Pacific company was formed under a Utah charter. The entire federal loan, including all interest, was paid to the U.S. government. E. H. Harriman, who already controlled the Illinois Central, soon became the dominant figure in the new management of the Union Pacific. Between 1898 and Harriman's death in 1909 over $100 million was spent in transforming the UP into the strongest railroad in the West. When C. P. Huntington died in 1900 the Union Pacific acquired the Southern Pacific, but this combination was dissolved in 1913 by the Supreme Court. After Harriman's death his two sons, Averell and Roland, and Robert S. Lovett, Harriman's good friend and legal advisor, were active in Union Pacific management for many years.

The Union Pacific served the nation well in both World War I and

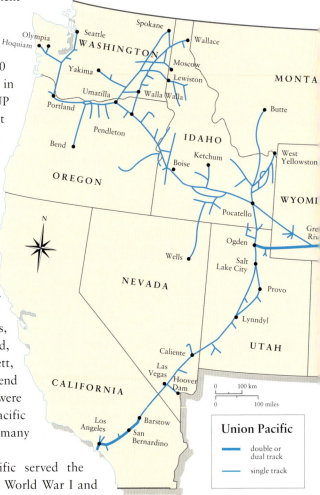

Union Pacific
- ▬▬ double or dual track
- ▬ single track

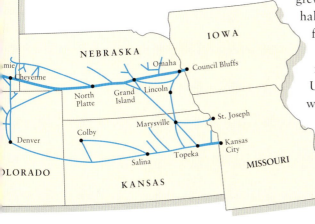

End of track, 1867, near Archer, Wyoming. Track supplies for building the Union Pacific arrived both by rail and by covered wagon.

World War II. Between 1941 and 1945 freight traffic climbed 83 percent and passenger traffic increased 195 percent. During the entire twentieth century the Union Pacific paid excellent dividends, even during the depression 1930s. The UP was a consistent winner in safety awards during these years. Especially after World War II the Union Pacific found the oil, gas, coal, and mineral deposits on its land-grant acres to be very profitable. The UP system grew during the first half of the century, from 2,900 miles in 1900 to 9,700 miles in 1950. In 1961 the UP sought to merge with the Rock Island. The ICC took thirteen years of hearings and delays to make up its mind, which pushed the Rock Island into its third and final bankruptcy in 1975. But the UP did acquire the Missouri Pacific and the Western Pacific in 1982, the Katy in 1988, and the Chicago and North Western in 1995. In 1996 the newly formed Surface Transportation Board approved the Union Pacific–Southern Pacific merger, creating a 35,000-mile system.

Southern Pacific

1950 Statistics	
(Moody's Railroads, 1951)	
Mileage	12,441
Number of states served	8
Freight revenue (millions)	$396
Passenger revenue (millions)	$39
Passenger revenue as % of freight revenue	10%
Total revenue (millions)	$470
Net income (millions)	$11
Operating ratio	73.1%
Employees	62,183
Workers per mile of line	4.9
Revenue per mile of line	$38,000
Locomotives	1,689
% diesel	21%
Freight cars	53,289
Passenger cars	1,379

The "Big Four"—Collis P. Huntington, Leland Stanford, Mark Hopkins, and Charles Crocker—started to build the Central Pacific in January 1863, two years before the start of any substantial work on the Union Pacific. They needed an early start because the high Sierras were a much rougher terrain than the Platte Valley in Nebraska and the mountains of Wyoming. After the 1869 Golden Spike the four men joined to plan and build the Southern Pacific Lines, a railroad to include the Central Pacific and to run the length of California and beyond. In the generation after 1869 the SP dominated rail services in California, and the high rail rates made the Big Four rich—rich enough for *American Heritage* in 1998 to list Huntington, Hopkins, and Stanford among the "forty wealthiest Americans of all time." A line was built north to Portland and others south to Los Angeles and Yuma. In 1883 a final spike was driven in West Texas joining the rails from Yuma with those going east to New Orleans.

In the 1880s and the 1890s Huntington, even though he had other rail interests in the East, was the dominant figure in the SP. In 1900 the Southern Pacific was a 7,500-mile line with yearly revenue of $60 million and an operating ratio of 65 percent. The 3,000 mile trip from Portland to New Orleans was the longest trip, without reversing general direction, that could be taken on any U.S. railway. The SP also owned a steamship line giving service between New

Orleans and New York City. During the Harriman control of the SP in the early twentieth century many improvements were made on the line, including the Lucin Cut-off across the Great Salt Lake.

Julius Kruttschnitt, an earlier lieutenant to Harriman, was chairman of the Southern Pacific from 1913 until his death in 1925. The SP was a prosperous railroad in the 1920s, paying regular 6 percent dividends. The depression 1930s were different, with freight tonnage in 1933 down to the level of 1906 and the employee roster only half that of the 1920s. The SP barely avoided receivership by drastically cutting costs. The wartime 1940s were so prosperous that the SP cut is funded debt by a quarter. The SP created its wholly owned Pacific Motor Trucking Company and also built its own oil pipeline from El Paso to Los Angeles. In 1965 *Forbes* claimed the SP was "one of the best run railroads in the U.S." In 1980 increased competition from both the Union Pacific and the Burlington Northern made the SP consider a merger with the Santa Fe, but the combination was not approved. By 1991 the Southern Pacific had merged with the smaller Denver and Rio Grande Western. Later, in 1996 the Southern Pacific was taken over by the Union Pacific.

Passenger traffic was excellent in the 1880s when this Southern Pacific train stopped at Los Gatos, California.

Santa Fe

1950 Statistics	
(Moody's Railroads, 1951)	
Mileage	13,073
Number of states served	12
Freight revenue (millions)	$422
Passenger revenue (millions)	$44
Passenger revenue as % of freight revenue	11%
Total revenue (millions)	$523
Net income (millions)	$82
Operating ratio	67.1%
Employees	61,426
Workers per mile of line	4.6
Revenue per mile of line	$40,000
Locomotives	2,022
% diesel	47%
Freight cars	80,367
Passenger cars	1,739

The Atchison, Topeka & Santa Fe Railway (the Santa Fe) was founded by Cyrus K. Holliday when he received a charter from Kansas in 1859. The U.S. Congress in 1863 provided a 3 million acre land grant for a rail route from Atchison west to the Colorado border. The line to Colorado was completed in 1872, and Pueblo, Colorado, was reached in 1876. In 1878 the Santa Fe officials cleverly outwitted their rival, the Denver & Rio Grande, and secured the vital Raton Pass into New Mexico. When the silver mines of Leadville became very productive in 1878 both roads sought to control the Royal Gorge route of the Arkansas River into the mountains and Leadville. Armed Santa Fe workers held the narrow gorge (too tight for two sets of tracks), but the U.S. Supreme Court finally ruled for the Rio Grande.

Denied the mountains of Colorado, the Santa Fe turned to New Mexico for a route to the Pacific. William Strong became president of the Santa Fe in 1881 and rapidly expanded the line by acquiring the Atlantic & Pacific, which had a federal land grant in the Southwest. By 1887 the Santa Fe had reached both Los Angeles and San Diego. Lines were also built into Texas and east to Chicago. In the 1870s and 1880s Santa Fe land-grant acres were widely sold in Kansas and other states. Beginning in 1876 Frederick H. Harvey provided fine railroad restaurants along the Santa Fe route. Soon hundreds of Harvey Girls, "Young women of good character, attractive and intelligent, 18 to 36," were serving the best food in the Southwest. Totally apocryphal is the story that Fred Harvey's dying words were, "Slice the ham thinner."

The Santa Fe had huge debts by the early

Ten minutes for lunch. Before the Santa Fe opened its Harvey Houses in 1876, meal stops could be hectic.

1890s and was in receivership by 1893. The reorganized line quickly recovered under Edward P. Ripley, president from 1896 to 1919. The Santa Fe in 1900 was a system of 7,425 miles, with revenue of $46 million and a 60 percent operating ratio. The Santa Fe paid regular dividends after 1901, even in the depression 1930s, except for 1933, 1938, and 1939. Santa Fe stock became a "blue chip," and some investors called the road "the Pennsylvania of the West." The Santa Fe stressed fine passenger service, and by midcentury the deluxe *Super Chief* gave 39.5 hour service between Chicago and Los Angeles (2,224 miles in 2,370 minutes). By midcentury the Santa Fe was first in mileage and third in operating revenue among all the railroads in the nation. In 1968 Santa Fe Industries was created as an umbrella for the railroad plus pipeline, oil, trucking, coal mining , and lumbering firms. Santa Fe was slow to seek mergers, but efforts to merge with the Western Pacific, and

later the Southern Pacific, were both rejected by the ICC. In 1995 the ICC, on a 4-0 vote, approved a merger with the Burlington Northern, thus creating the Burlington Northern Santa Fe Corporation, a system of 35,000 miles.

Atchison, Topeka & Santa Fe

— double or dual track   — single track

Northern Pacific

1950 Statistics	
(Moody's Railroads, 1951)	
Mileage	6,904
Number of states served	7
Freight revenue (millions)	$147
Passenger revenue (millions)	$6
Passenger revenue as % of freight revenue	4%
Total revenue (millions)	$167
Net income (millions)	$20
Operating ratio	72.9%
Employees	24,555
Workers per mile of line	3.5
Revenue per mile of line	$23,000
Locomotives	771
% diesel	14%
Freight cars	37,111
Passenger cars	578

The Northern Pacific Railroad, the second complete transcontinental route, was created by an act of Congress on July 2, 1864. The act provided for a line from Lake Superior to the Pacific Northwest, with twenty sections of land for each mile built in a state, and forty sections per mile in western territories. The route's terrain was bleak, the population sparse, and the rate of construction slow. Josiah Perham, a Yankee showman and the NP president, failed in his dream that the common people would rush to finance the project. It remained for Jay Cooke, Philadelphia banker and successful salesman of Civil War bonds, to finance construction of the NP. Building started in 1870, and by 1873 500 miles had been opened to Bismarck, North Dakota.

In the fall of 1873 Jay Cooke's bank closed its doors, a financial panic swept the nation, and construction of the NP came to a halt. Congress refused any aid because of the Credit Mobilier scandal. Henry Villard, an immigrant from Bavaria and a Civil War press correspondent, became interested in western railroads. With help from fellow investors Villard purchased the NP in 1879. Large construction crews, many of them from China, completed the Northern Pacific. In 1883, west of Helena, Montana, the last rails were laid in the presence of President Chester A. Arthur and General U. S. Grant. Later independent branch lines and a road to Seattle were added.

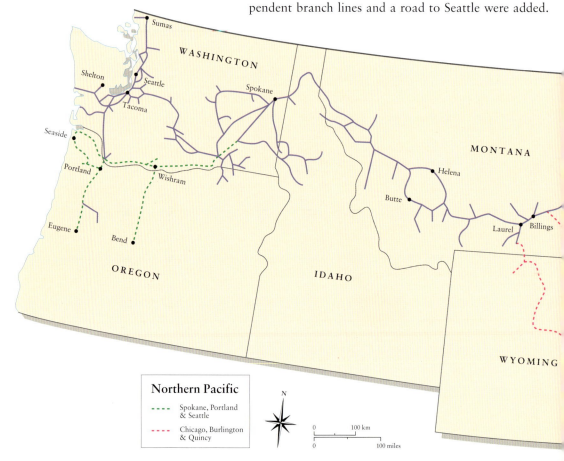

Northern Pacific

- - - Spokane, Portland & Seattle
- - - Chicago, Burlington & Quincy

N

0   100 km

0   100 miles

The NP was in financial trouble in the 1880s, and with the Panic of 1893 the road was soon in receivership. In the reorganization that followed, James J. Hill gained a major interest in the Northern Pacific. In 1900 the NP was a system of 4,700 miles with annual revenue of $30 million.

Improvements in NP motive force, rolling stock, and physical plant were made in the early twentieth century. Heavy World War I traffic at the lower land-grant rates placed a heavy strain on the Northern Pacific. In the 1920s the Northern Pacific replaced branch line passenger trains with small gas-electric units. The depression 1930s were difficult years for the NP. There were days in that period when a single freight train, each way, took care of the limited traffic. The problem was made worse by an agricultural slump and poor crop years in the NP region. The years of World War II were much better for the Northern Pacific, and the road's financial condition was much improved by the mid-1940s. The NP was reluctant to shift quickly to diesels because it had at mid-century a modern fleet of steam locomotives. The switch to diesel power on the NP was only made complete in 1957. The long-sought merger of the Hill roads was made in 1970 with the ICC approval and creation of the Burlington Northern System (the Northern Pacific; the Great Northern; the Chicago, Burlington & Quincy; and the Spokane, Portland & Seattle).

Great Northern

1950 Statistics	
(Moody's Railroads, 1951)	
Mileage	8,316
Number of states served	10
Freight revenue (millions)	$196
Passenger revenue (millions)	$11
Passenger revenue as % of freight revenue	6%
Total revenue (millions)	$227
Net income (millions)	$28
Operating ratio	71.3%
Employees	28,490
Workers per mile of line	3.9
Revenue per mile of line	$28,000
Locomotives	1,012
% diesel	42%
Freight cars	38,315
Passenger cars	822

The first railroad that became a part of the Great Northern Railway was the Minnesota & Pacific, chartered in 1857. After defaulting, the M&P was reorganized as the St. Paul & Pacific. The newly named road was a short 10 miles of track along the upper Mississippi from St. Paul to

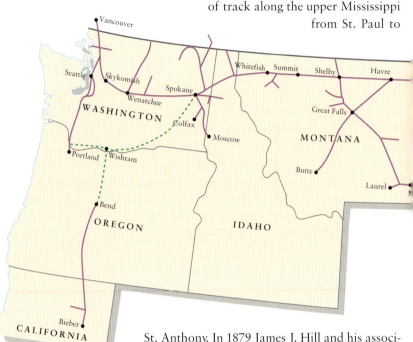

St. Anthony. In 1879 James J. Hill and his associates reorganized the St. Paul & Pacific as the St. Paul, Minneapolis & Manitoba Railway. Jim Hill, born in Canada, had arrived in St. Paul in 1856 at the age of seventeen. His first job was as a $2-a-day clerk/laborer for a steamboat line, but a decade later he had his own fleet of boats. In the 1860s and 1870s Hill had had a varied experience in frontier freighting and transportation.

Hill and his friends built their railroad, which critics called "Hill's Folly," north along the Red River to Winnipeg. Jim Hill was blind in his right eye, but his vision concerning the future of western railroading was nearly 20/20. In 1889 Hill and his friends renamed their railroad the Great Northern and turned its direction westward toward the Pacific. The GN was located north of the Northern Pacific quite close to the Canadian border. Hill directed his locating engineer, John F. Stevens, to build slowly and carefully with low grades and few sharp curves. When the GN reached Seattle in 1893 it was one of the best-built railroads in the West, and it had been built without any land-grant aid from the government. The Panic of 1893 pushed many western roads into receivership, but not the GN. Between 1894 and 1900 the 3,800-mile GN had an average operating ration of 52 percent and paid yearly dividends of 5 to 7 percent.

Early in the twentieth century both Hill and Harriman sought to acquire the Chicago, Burlington & Quincy, as an entry into Chicago. Hill won the hectic stock market battle and created the Northern Securities Company to control the Great Northern, the Burlington, and his earlier acquisition, the Northern Pacific. In 1904 the Supreme Court ruled that each of the three roads would have to be operated separately. The Great Northern was a very prosperous road during the entire twentieth century. Jim Hill supported agriculture with gifts of

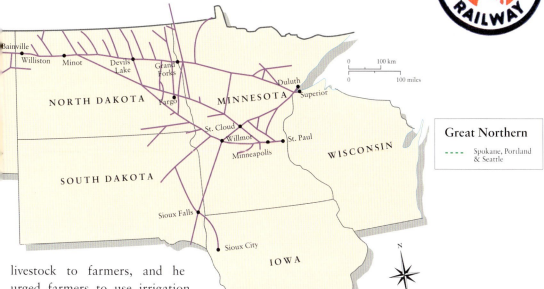

Great Northern

- - - - Spokane, Portland & Seattle

livestock to farmers, and he urged farmers to use irrigation and to add dairying to the growing of wheat. GN depots often had cord wood lots nearby so that farm wagons bringing wheat to market need not return home empty. Jim Hill did not greatly favor passenger traffic, but the GN did provide excellent passenger service on both the *Oriental Limited* and the *Empire Builder*. In 1929 the new 8-mile *Cascade* Tunnel was opened in Washington. The GN shifted to diesel motive power after World War II faster than many western lines. In 1970 the ICC made Hill's dream of a large rail system come true with the creation of the Burlington Northern merger (GN, NP, CB&Q, and the Spokane, Portland & Seattle). In 1971 the GN route west was included in the new Amtrak passenger service.

Snow Bound. American Railroad Scene. *(Currier & Ives print). There were reports that one of the workers digging out the train was James J. Hill.*

Chicago, Burlington & Quincy

1950 Statistics	
(Moody's Railroads, 1951)	
Mileage	10,762
Number of states served	13
Freight revenue (millions)	$230
Passenger revenue (millions)	$20
Passenger revenue as % of freight revenue	8%
Total revenue (millions)	$280
Net income (millions)	$34
Operating ratio	66%
Employees	33,500
Workers per mile of line	3.1
Revenue per mile of line	$27,000
Locomotives	1,249
% diesel	39%
Freight cars	46,799
Passenger cars	1,155

The Chicago, Burlington & Quincy (often called the Burlington), one of the four major Granger Roads, was an 1856 merger of four short lines near Chicago—the Aurora Branch, the Northern Cross, the Peoria & Oquawka, and the Central Military Tract. Investors in the Michigan Central, including John Murray Forbes of Boston, were in charge of the new CB&Q. John Forbes, a man of strong principles and the highest integrity, gave guidance to the Burlington for its first four decades. Thus the CB&Q was a strong road; it has never been close to receivership and has paid dividends every year since the Civil War. By 1860 the 210-mile CB&Q had a revenue of $1.5 million and paid its first dividend. The Burlington, aided by a land grant, built a line across Iowa to the Missouri River by 1870.

In the 1870s and 1880s, Burlington salesmen sold thousands of land grant acres in southern Iowa, northern Missouri, and eastern Nebraska to would-be farmers coming from eastern states and western Europe. The land was often sold with ten year's credit at about six percent interest, with the price set according to the nature of the soil, the proximity to the railroad, and the availability of timber and water. Prices ranged from six to ten dollars per acre, with a discount given for a cash sale. In Nebraska between 1870 and 1890, the growth of the state's population and the mileage of new railroads climbed at about the same rate.

Charles E. Perkins, Forbes's cousin, was the CB&Q president from 1881 to 1901 and in the twenty years nearly tripled the road's mileage. By 1882 the CB&Q had acquired the Hannibal & St. Joe, a line across northern Missouri, and had built a road across Nebraska to Denver. A line up the Mississippi to St. Paul was opened in 1886. By 1894 the system reached St. Louis, and a branch was built north into Montana to connect with the Northern Pacific. In 1900 the Burlington was a 7,600-mile system, with revenue of $41 million, an operating ratio of 62 percent, and dividends of 6 percent.

In 1901 Jim Hill won his struggle with Harriman over the control of the Burlington, but a 1904 Supreme Court ruling forced the Burlington to be operated as an independent line. In 1908 the Burlington gained control of the Colorado & Southern, which had lines from Denver south to Fort Worth and Galveston. The Burlington aided midwestern agriculture with experimental dry farms, seed corn lecture trains, and research projects in agricultural schools in Nebraska, Iowa, and Missouri. During Ralph Budd's years as president, 1932 to 1949, streamlined Zephyrs and popular Vista-Dome passenger cars appeared. By 1947 nearly all through freight trains and all named passenger trains from Chicago to the Twin Cities and Denver were powered by diesels. By 1956 Slumbercoach service was introduced on the new *Denver Zephyr*. In 1970 the ICC finally approved Jim Hill's dream of a giant merger when the new Burlington Northern included the CB&Q, the Great Northern, the Northern Pacific, and the Spokane, Portland & Seattle. Still later the ICC approved a merger with the Santa Fe, creating in 1995 the Burlington Northern Santa Fe Corporation.

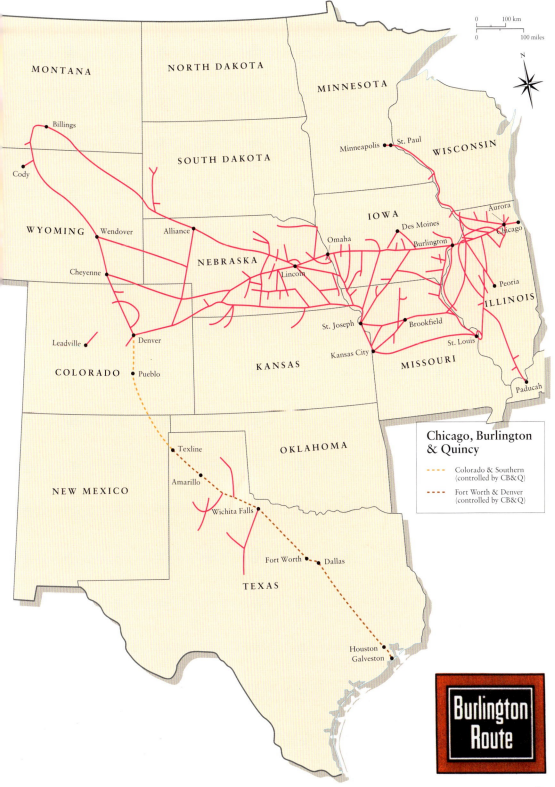

MONTANA

NORTH DAKOTA

MINNESOTA

WISCONSIN

SOUTH DAKOTA

Minneapolis • St. Paul

Billings

Cody

WYOMING

Wendover

Alliance

Cheyenne

NEBRASKA

Lincoln

IOWA

Des Moines

Omaha

Burlington

Aurora

Chicago

Peoria

ILLINOIS

St. Joseph

Brookfield

Leadville

Denver

KANSAS

Kansas City

St. Louis

MISSOURI

COLORADO

Pueblo

Paducah

NEW MEXICO

Texline

OKLAHOMA

Amarillo

Wichita Falls

Fort Worth • Dallas

TEXAS

Houston
Galveston

Chicago, Burlington & Quincy

- - - - - Colorado & Southern
(controlled by CB&Q)

- - - - - Fort Worth & Denver
(controlled by CB&Q)

Burlington Route

Chicago, Rock Island & Pacific

1950 Statistics	
(Moody's Railroads, 1951)	
Mileage	7,610
Number of states served	14
Freight revenue (millions)	$144
Passenger revenue (millions)	$18
Passenger revenue as % of freight revenue	13%
Total revenue (millions)	$180
Net income (millions)	$18
Operating ratio	72.8%
Employees	21,841
Workers per mile of line	2.9
Revenue per mile of line	$24,000
Locomotives	742
% diesel	44%
Freight cars	27,500
Passenger cars	782

In February 1851 the Chicago & Rock Island Railroad (often called the Rock Island), another Granger railroad, was given a charter by the Illinois legislature. In 1852 the line was built to Joliet, and the entire 181-mile route from Chicago to Rock Island was finished by 1854. Henry Farnam, a self-taught surveyor from New York, had completed the Rock Island ahead of schedule and by 1856 had also constructed a six-span bridge over the Mississippi River. Only two weeks after the opening of the bridge, the central span was destroyed by fire, having been hit by the steamboat *Effie Afton*. Abraham Lincoln won the resulting lawsuit for the Rock Island with his claim that "people have as much right to travel east and west as north and south."

The Rock Island later merged with the Mississippi & Missouri Railroad in 1866 to form the Chicago, Rock Island & Pacific. The newly merged road reached Omaha in May 1869. The Rock Island sold most of its Iowa land grant to settlers for $7.00 to $8.00 an acre. In 1875 the Rock Island was a 675-mile road with a yearly revenue of $7 million and an operating ratio of 52 percent. In the post–Civil War years the road was paying dividends of $7.00 or $8.00 a year. In 1880 the Rock Island was the only line between Chicago and the Missouri River with an all-steel track. By 1900 a larger Rock Island had 3,600 miles, revenue of $23 million, and an operating ration of 62 percent. In the late 1880s dividends were 2 to 4 percent a year.

In 1901 the Rock Island was taken over by the Reid-Moore Syndicate, a group of four or five unscrupulous stock speculators who spent several million dollars for a large block of Rock Island common stock. The gang increased the capital stock by 20 percent and embarked on a costly and reckless expansion. The problem was made worse by the high operating costs and low freight rates faced by all railroads. The Rock Island was in receivership by 1914. Its financial problems were still present in the 1920s, and the line was bankrupt again in 1933.

In 1936 John D. Farrington became the chief operating officer on the Rock Island and was president or board chairman from 1942 to 1961. Farrington rehabilitated the entire railroad and introduced diesel-powered passenger trains and Rocket streamliners. The road's operating ratio dropped from 89 percent in 1935 to 75 percent in 1955. The Rock Island entered the 1950s with optimism but still faced stiff competition from truck, airlines, and other railroads. In the early 1960s the Union Pacific proposed a merger with the Rock Island. The ICC took a dozen years for hearings with long delays, pushing the Rock Island into a third and final bankruptcy in 1975. The Rock Island shut down in 1980 and was liquidated.

Rock Island Bridge, built over the Mississippi in 1856. The bridge was destroyed two weeks later when hit by a steamboat.

Chicago, Rock Island & Pacific

Chicago & North Western

1950 Statistics	
(Moody's Railroads, 1951)	
Mileage	7,992
Number of states served	8
Freight revenue (millions)	$146
Passenger revenue (millions)	$21
Passenger revenue as % of freight revenue	14%
Total revenue (millions)	$189
Net income (millions)	$5
Operating ratio	84%
Employees	25,877
Workers per mile of line	3.6
Revenue per mile of line	$24,000
Locomotives	1,072
% diesel	31%
Freight cars	44,169
Passenger cars	1,110

A predecessor line to the Chicago & North Western (often called the North Western), the Galena & Chicago Union, started construction in 1848. By 1850 it was open to Elgin, 42 miles west of Chicago and was grossing $1,000 a week. William Butler Ogden, Chicago's first mayor, was president of the short line. Later Ogden built a railroad north of Chicago into Wisconsin, which in 1859 became the Chicago & North Western. In 1864 the North Western acquired the Galena & Chicago Union. The North Western also had a line in Iowa, west of Clinton, that was extended in 1867 to Council Bluffs, where it was the first road from Chicago to connect with the Union Pacific.

Granger-backed legislation in the 1870s in Illinois, Iowa, and Wisconsin was critical of all railroads, including the North Western. But most midwestern farmers admitted that the North Western gave good service and had fair freight rates. During the presidency of Marvin Hughitt, 1887 to 1910, the line greatly expanded its mileage and also prospered. The railroad had little difficulty with its employees, having no serious trouble during the 1877 strike or the 1894 Pullman Strike. In 1900 the North Western was a system of 5,300 miles with revenue of $42 million and an operating ratio of 60 percent. From 1894 to 1900 it paid yearly dividends that averaged just over 5 percent. At the turn of the century the line was widely known as the railroad with "the best of every-

thing." In the last years of the nineteenth century the North Western, along with the Union Pacific and the Southern Pacific, ran the "Overland Flyer" from Chicago to San Francisco. Later the name was changed to "Overland Limited."

The North Western faced stiff competition in the 1920s from trucks, automobiles, and intercity bus lines. The depression of the 1930s finally forced the line into bankruptcy in 1935. The line was reorganized in the early 1940s, and World War II traffic brought a measure of prosperity. In 1956 Ben W. Heineman became the chief operating officer. He quickly streamlined operations, abandoned some branch lines, and in time made the Chicago commuter service profitable. In the early 1970s Heineman sold the Chicago & North Western to the line's employees. In recent years the North Western has built new mileage in Nebraska and Wyoming to tap the coal traffic (unit train) from the South Powder River Basin. Following the shutdown of the Rock Island the North Western purchased some short segments of that road, including the rail route from the Twin Cities south to Kansas City. In 1995 the Union Pacific purchased the great majority of the capital stock of the Chicago & North Western, bringing it completely under Union Pacific control.

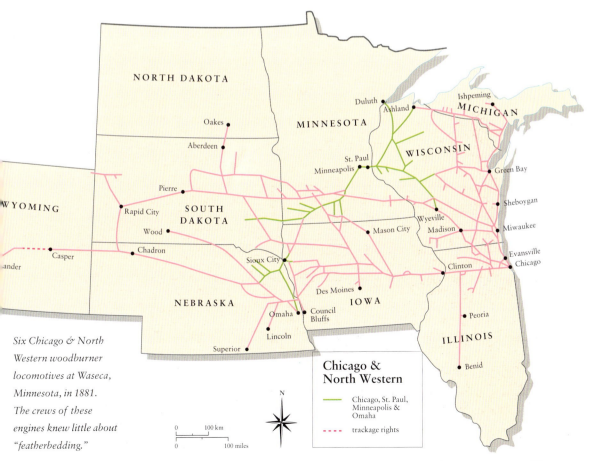

Six Chicago & North Western woodburner locomotives at Waseca, Minnesota, in 1881. The crews of these engines knew little about "featherbedding."

Chicago &
North Western

— Chicago, St. Paul, Minneapolis & Omaha

- - - trackage rights

Chicago, Milwaukee, St. Paul & Pacific

1950 Statistics	
(Moody's Railroads, 1951)	
Mileage	10,671
Number of states served	14
Freight revenue (millions)	$210
Passenger revenue (millions)	$18
Passenger revenue as % of freight revenue	9%
Total revenue (millions)	$255
Net income (millions)	$14
Operating ratio	78.2%
Employees	33,668
Workers per mile of line	3.1
Revenue per mile of line	$24,000
Locomotives	1,308
% diesel	27%
Freight cars	58,787
Passenger cars	1,132

The last of the four Granger lines was the Chicago, Milwaukee, St. Paul & Pacific, often known as the Milwaukee. Byron Kilbourn, the mayor of Milwaukee, was president of the Milwaukee and Mississippi, a line originally chartered in 1847. Kilbourn dreamed to see Milwaukee rival and even surpass Chicago, but in 1851 his short line ended 20 miles west of Milwaukee. The extension of the M&M to Prairie du Chien in 1857 was partially financed by an ingenious farm mortgage stock purchase plan. Unhappily, after the 1857 Panic many farmers lost their farms; some had never lived near a railroad, and all became active Grange members.

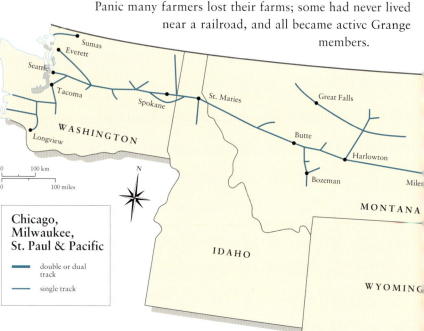

Chicago,
Milwaukee,
St. Paul & Pacific

— double or dual track

— single track

In 1863 the Milwaukee & St. Paul Railway was organized out of the Milwaukee & Mississippi and several other short Wisconsin lines. Alexander Mitchell, a Scotch immigrant who became a prosperous Milwaukee banker, was president of the Milwaukee & St. Paul from 1865 to 1887. By 1869 the Milwaukee was an 830-mile system with a line up to St. Paul. The road reached Chicago in 1873, and in 1874 its name became Chicago, Milwaukee & St. Paul. By 1886 the Milwaukee was a 5,000-mile road with an annual revenue of $24 million and an operating ratio of 58 percent; it was a payer of regular dividends. In 1900 the Milwaukee was known for its sound finances and capable management.

Albert J. Earling, president of the Milwaukee from 1899 to 1917, decided to make his Granger line into the third transcontinental in the Northwest. A 1,400-mile extension from South Dakota to Seattle was built between 1905 and 1909, and "& Pacific" was added to the line's name. More than 600 miles of the new route—in Montana, Idaho, and Washington—was electrified between 1916 and the mid-1920s. Both the extended route construction and the shift to electric motive power cost far more than the original estimates, and the debt was tripled by 1923. The expected boom in traffic never appeared, partly because of an economic slump in the Northwest and the opening of the Panama Canal in 1914. The Milwaukee common stock, listed at $200 in 1905, dropped to $4 in 1925 when the line slipped into bankruptcy.

The Milwaukee emerged from receivership in 1928, but the depression of the 1930s forced it again into bankruptcy in 1935. A high-speed streamliner, the *Hiawatha*, gave excellent service between Chicago and the Twin Cities in the 1930s. After a 1945 reorganization other *Hiawathas* served Chicago, Omaha, and Seattle. The 1970 merger of the Great Northern, the Northern

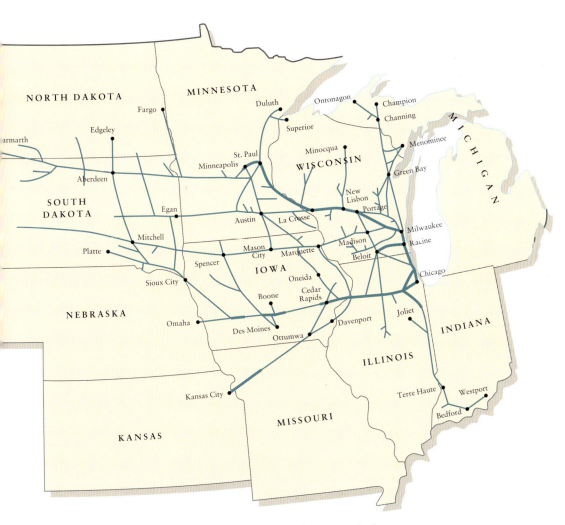

Pacific, and the Burlington into the Burlington Northern was bad news for the Milwaukee. The electrification of the Pacific extension was phased out in the early 1970s, and the road's final bankruptcy came in 1977. Thousands of miles of line were abandoned, and what remained was sold in 1986 to the Soo Line.

New York, New Haven & Hartford

1950 Statistics	
(Moody's Railroads, 1951)	
Mileage	1,794
Number of states served	4
Freight revenue (millions)	$89
Passenger revenue (millions)	$47
Passenger revenue as % of freight revenue	52%
Total revenue (millions)	$150
Net income (millions)	$11
Operating ratio	76.3%
Employees	21,402
Workers per mile of line	11.9
Revenue per mile of line	$84,000
Locomotives	530
% diesel	63%
% electric	20%
Freight cars	8,589
Passenger cars	1,498

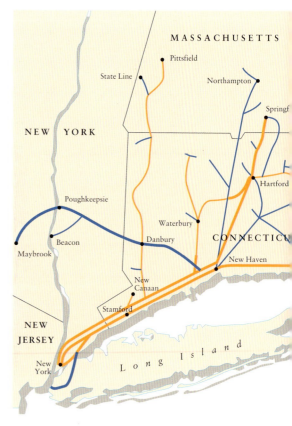

The New York & New Haven Railroad was incorporated by Connecticut in 1844, and the 63-mile line was completed in 1848. In the early years passenger revenue was two or three times as large as freight revenue. The prosperity of the road was cut short in 1853 when the early-morning express train ran through an open drawbridge, causing a death toll of forty-two and a half-million dollar damage suit. A year later it was discovered that the road's president, Robert Schuyler, a nephew of Alexander Hamilton, had illegally issued $2 million of company stock and then fled the country. A second line, the 78-mile Hartford & New Haven, chartered in 1833, was finished by mid-century. Both roads prospered and, despite opposition within the state, were merged in 1872 as the New York, New Haven & Hartford, often called the New Haven.

New Haven 9:45. Accommodation train at Stratford, Connecticut. This 1867 painting by E. L. Henry showed the role village depots played a long century ago.

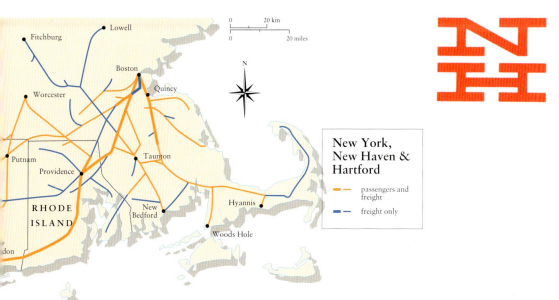

In 1885 the New Haven was a 265-mile line, located chiefly in Connecticut, with $4 million of passenger revenue and $2.5 million of freight revenue. Its operating ratio was 67 percent, and it paid annual dividends of $1.5 million. Charles P. Clark, former U.S. Naval officer in the Civil War who was in foreign trade before entering railroading, was the New Haven president from 1887 to 1899. In the dozen years the New Haven leased and absorbed many short lines in southern New England, and by 1900 it was operating over 2,000 miles of road in Connecticut, Massachusetts, and Rhode Island. Clark hoped to control all the railways between New York City and Boston. By 1900 freight revenue surpassed passenger by 10 percent. In that year the New Haven revenue was $40 million, the operating ratio 70 percent, and the dividends $4 million.

After 1900 J. P. Morgan and his bank controlled the enlarged New Haven. Morgan selected Charles S. Mellen, formerly president of the Northern Pacific, to be president of the New Haven. Mellen continued to expand the New Haven, including many short trolley lines in southern New England. The new president also electrified the New York to New Haven line and constructed the Hill Gate Bridge near New York City. Later Mellen, and indirectly J. P. Morgan, were censored by the ICC for monopolistic practices and neglecting proper maintenance of the road. In 1913 Mellen resigned as president of the New Haven and J. P. Morgan died.

In the 1920s the poor financial condition of the New Haven did not improve. The New Haven went bankrupt in 1935, and the difficult reorganization was not complete until 1948. The bad financial condition of the New Haven continued in the 1950s and 1960s. The ICC insisted that any merger of the New York Central and the Pennsylvania had to include the New Haven. The New Haven was included in the creation of the Penn Central in 1969.

Missouri Pacific

1950 Statistics	
(Moody's Railroads, 1951)	
Mileage	6,444
Number of states served	8
Freight revenue (millions)	$186
Passenger revenue (millions)	$11
Passenger revenue as % of freight revenue	6%
Total revenue (millions)	$200
Net income (millions)	$17
Operating ratio	73.2%
Employees	28,351
Workers per mile of line	4.4
Revenue per mile of line	$39,000
Locomotives	863
% diesel	34%
Freight cars	36,226
Passenger cars	513

The first locomotive west of the Mississippi, the Pacific, was shipped by steamboat from New Orleans to St. Louis in 1852. Later it was operated by the Missouri Pacific Railroad.

The Pacific Railroad of Missouri received a state charter on March 12, 1849, to build a railway across the state from St. Louis to the Kansas border. Senator Thomas Hart Benton of Missouri was a major proponent of the projected line. The *Pacific*, the first locomotive west of the Mississippi, arrived in St. Louis in August 1852, coming via steamboat from New Orleans. The new engine operated over the first 6 miles of line west of St. Louis in December 1852. Construction was slow, but 214 miles of road were finished by the end of the Civil War. The road reached Kansas City by 1867, and an "Express" passenger train had a scheduled 15-hour, 40-minute run for the 283 miles between St. Louis and Kansas City, or an average of 18 miles per hour. In 1876 the Pacific of Missouri was reorganized as the Missouri Pacific Railway.

Jay Gould controlled the Missouri Pacific from 1879 to 1892. The MP served as a "home base" for his competition with the Burlington to the north and the Denver & Rio Grande and the Santa Fe to the west. Gould soon was leasing or absorbing several nearby roads, such as the St. Louis, Iron Mountain & Southern. By 1887 the enlarged Missouri Pacific was a 4,100-mile system extending from St. Louis and Omaha west and south to Pueblo, El Paso, Memphis, and New Orleans. Jay Gould's reputation as a "wrecker" of railroads did not apply to his management of the Missouri Pacific. This hub or home-base railroad of his expanding southwestern rail system was well managed and maintained during the dozen years of Gould control. Jay Gould's son, George, was president of the MP after Jay's death in 1892. The Missouri Pacific did not fare as well during George Gould's reign.

The Missouri Pacific did not prosper in the early twentieth century. In 1917 the St. Louis & Iron Mountain was merged with the MP. During the 1920s the Van Sweringen brothers became interested in the Missouri Pacific, but by 1933

the line was bankrupt, a receivership that did not end until 1956. From 1961 until 1983 Downing B. Jenks, former Rock Island president, was president or chairman of the MP. During his years many improvements were made on the Missouri Pacific. Both motive power and rolling stock were revamped and standardized. He reduced and finally shut down all passenger service and greatly increased the use of computers. By 1980 the Missouri Pacific was a well-managed railroad. In 1982 the Union Pacific added the MP to its expanding rail empire.

Missouri Pacific

Gulf, Mobile & Ohio

1950 Statistics	
(Moody's Railroads, 1951)	
Mileage	2,898
Number of states served	7
Freight revenue (millions)	$67
Passenger revenue (millions)	$5
Passenger revenue as % of freight revenue	7%
Total revenue (millions)	$78
Net income (millions)	$8
Operating ratio	70.3%
Employees	9,779
Workers per mile of line	3.4
Revenue per mile of line	$26,000
Locomotives	240
% diesel	100%
Freight cars	11,767
Passenger cars	207

The Mobile & Ohio Railroad was chartered in 1848 when the business interests of Mobile became worried about the decline of commerce in their city. In 1850 the land-grant act, sponsored by U. S. Senators William R. King of Alabama and Stephen A. Douglas of Illinois, provided 1,147,000 acres of land in Mississippi and Alabama for the projected lines. By 1856 the M&O had built 198 miles of road, and the entire 483-mile route from Mobile north to Columbus, Kentucky, was completed in April 1861. A 20-mile steamboat route north to Cairo, Illinois, connected the M&O with the Illinois Central. Wartime damage kept the M&O busy in the late 1860s and was so costly that the road fell into receivership in 1875. The Mobile & Ohio reached East Cairo in 1882, and the Illinois Central built a bridge over the Ohio in 1889. The Mobile & Ohio in 1900 operated 876 miles of line, had a yearly revenue of $6 million, and had an operating ratio of 70 percent. The Southern Railway acquired control of the M&O in 1901, but the M&O continued to have an independent operation.

Another predecessor company of the Gulf, Mobile & Ohio was the Gulf, Mobile & Northern, chartered several years after the Civil War. The Gulf, Mobile & Northern prospered during the 1920s and 1930s during the presidency of Isaac B. Tigrett. By 1927 the G,M&N operated about 1,000 miles of road, located mainly in Alabama and Mississippi. In the 1930s the Gulf, Mobile & Northern sought to acquire the Mobile & Ohio in order to gain a northern connection to trunk-line railroads. The Southern Railway relinquished its control of the M&O to the G,M&N in the late 1930s.

In 1940 the Gulf, Mobile & Northern and the Mobile & Ohio were merged to form the Gulf, Mobile & Ohio, a system with about 2,000 miles of road from St. Louis south to Mobile and New Orleans. The newly merged railroad prospered during World War II. In 1947 the G,M&O acquired the ailing Alton Railroad, which operated a line from Chicago via St. Louis to Kansas City. In 1972 the Gulf, Mobile & Ohio merged with the larger Illinois Central to form the 9,500-mile Illinois Central Gulf.

The Mississippi, *the first locomotive in Mississippi, arrived in the state late in 1836.*

Chicago
Joliet
Peoria
Bloomington
Springfield
Roodhouse
ILLINOIS
Slater
Mexico
Kansas
City
MISSOURI
St. Louis
East St. Louis
Murphysboro
Tamms
KENTUCKY
Jackson
TENNESSEE
Memphis
Corinth
ARKANSAS
Artesia
Birmingham
MISSISSIPPI
Union
Meridian
Montgomery
ALABAMA
Bogalusa
Mobile
LOUISIANA
New Orleans

0   100 km
0   100 miles

N

Gulf, Mobile & Ohio

- - - -   trackage rights

Missouri, Kansas & Texas

1950 Statistics	
(Moody's Railroads, 1951)	
Mileage	3,243
Number of states served	4
Freight revenue (millions)	$65
Passenger revenue (millions)	$5
Passenger revenue as % of freight revenue	8%
Total revenue (millions)	$78
Net income (millions)	$6
Operating ratio	71.2%
Employees	10,275
Workers per mile of line	3.2
Revenue per mile of line	$24,000
Locomotives	252
% diesel	30%
Freight cars	8,738
Passenger cars	182

The Missouri, Kansas & Texas Railway, often known as the Katy, was formed in 1870 as the successor to the Union Pacific Southern Branch, which had been incorporated in 1865. Judge Levi Parsons, a lawyer from New York by way of California, was president of the Katy from 1868 until 1874. The road was built in the shape of a shallow "V" from Junction City, Kansas, and Sedalia, Missouri, south to Parsons, Kansas, in the southeastern corner of the state. Both lines reached Parsons by the spring of 1871. The Katy was the first railroad to enter the Indian Territory (now Oklahoma), and a line was completed south from Parsons to Denison, Texas, by early 1873.

The depression following the Panic of 1873 forced the Katy into receivership late in 1874. The Katy was reorganized in 1876 and in 1880 was leased to Jay Gould's Missouri Pacific, with the rental being the annual net earnings. In 1880 the Katy was an 880-mile line with yearly revenue of about $4 million. By 1886 it had grown to 1,386 miles with extensions built to Hannibal, Missouri, and Ft. Worth and Dallas, Texas. By 1888 the capital stock was far more widely held than a decade earlier. In the annual meeting of 1888 the Gould regime was met with cries of, "Throw the scalawags out." The lease was canceled, and a new board of directors was elected.

Shortly after Gould's departure the two Oklahoma District "runs" of April 22, 1889, and September 16, 1893, took place. The Katy in the 1890s and early twentieth century continued to extend its lines—to Kansas City and St. Louis in the north and to San Antonio and Houston in Texas. The Katy's mileage was up to 4,000 miles by 1915. The railroad suffered another receivership in 1915 and was not fully reorganized until 1923. The Katy did manage to escape receivership in the 1930s depression. World War II brought prosperity to the Katy, but in the 1950s the line suffered from a huge capital and debt structure. Donald V. Fraser, a longtime Katy employee, was president or chairman of the Katy from 1945 to 1961, but did little to improve or upgrade the service or finances of the road. John W. Barriger III, president in the late 1960s, did manage to abandon some branch-line service and improve the remaining routes. By the 1980s the Katy was an obvious candidate for an appropriate merger. In 1988 the Union Pacific acquired the Missouri, Kansas & Texas for its expanding rail empire.

Jay Gould. Gould treated a few railroads well, but the other stockholders of the Katy were not happy with his control.

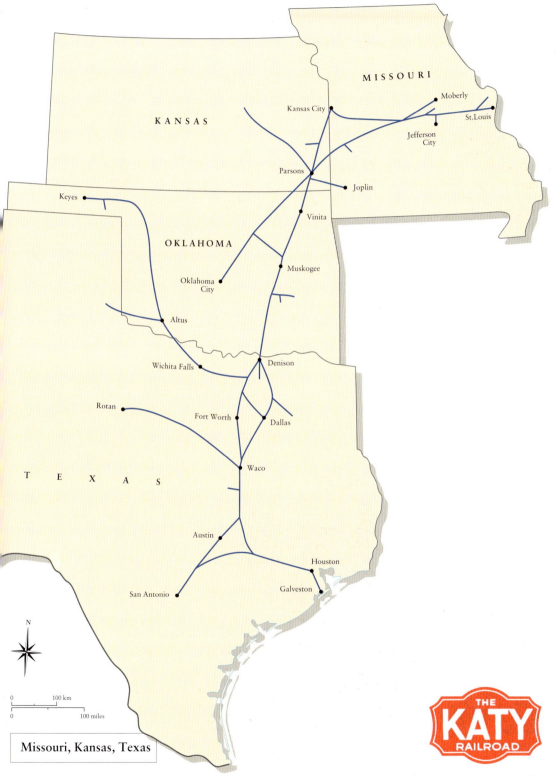

KANSAS

MISSOURI

Kansas City

Moberly

St. Louis

Jefferson City

Parsons

Joplin

Keyes

Vinita

OKLAHOMA

Muskogee

Oklahoma City

Altus

Wichita Falls

Denison

Rotan

Fort Worth

Dallas

Waco

T E X A S

Austin

Houston

San Antonio

Galveston

N

0   100 km

0   100 miles

Missouri, Kansas, Texas

THE KATY RAILROAD

Denver & Rio Grande Western

1950 Statistics	
(Moody's Railroads, 1951)	
Mileage	2,366
Number of states served	3
Freight revenue (millions)	$60
Passenger revenue (millions)	$3
Passenger revenue as % of freight revenue	5%
Total revenue (millions)	$66
Net income (millions)	$6
Operating ratio	71.3%
Employees	7,938
Workers per mile of line	3.3
Revenue per mile of line	$28,000
Locomotives	392
% diesel	43%
Freight cars	13,972
Passenger cars	173

The Denver & Rio Grande Railway was organized in the Colorado Territory in October 1870 to build a line from Denver south through New Mexico to El Paso, Texas. General William J. Palmer, Civil War veteran and builder of the Kansas Pacific in the late 1860s, was president of the new road. The Rio Grande was to be a 3-foot, narrow-gauge line: a road with less expensive cars and motive power, with tighter curves and steeper grades than standard gauge. By 1873 the road was built to Pueblo, 155 miles south of Denver. In 1878 the Santa Fe occupied the Raton Pass and thus denied Palmer's line a chance to build south into New Mexico. The Santa Fe also violently challenged the efforts of the D&RG to build westward up the Arkansas River. However, the U.S. Supreme Court in 1879 and 1880 finally decided in favor of the Rio Grande. By 1882 the Rio Grande had built nearly a thousand miles of line in Colorado and had reached Durango, Leadville, and the Utah state line.

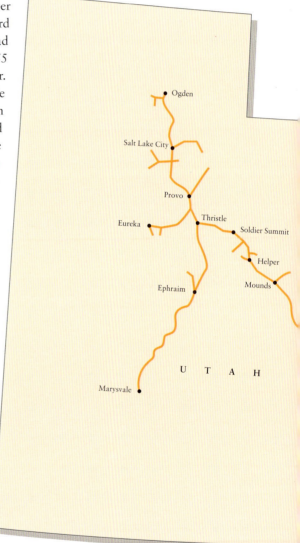

Palmer gave up the presidency of the Denver & Rio Grande in 1883 when Gould threatened his road. Earlier Palmer had organized the Denver & Rio Grande Western, which would build a line from the Colorado–Utah border to Salt Lake City. In the 1880s some of the major routes of the D&RG had added a third outside rail to their track to accommodate standard-gauge equipment. In 1901 George Gould, son of Jay, had acquired both the D&RG and the D&RGW, which he operated together. Later George

Gould started the Western Pacific from Salt Lake City to Oakland, which saddled the D&RGW with a heavy debt.

During the early twentieth century the D&RGW changed most of its line to standard gauge and abandoned much of the remaining narrow gauge. The road's general neglect, huge debt, and mismanagement made some of its critics call the road the "Dangerous & Rapidly Growing Worse." The completion of the Moffat Tunnel and the Dotsero Cutoff in 1934 gave Denver and the railroad a new route to the west. The *California Zephyr*, operated by the Burlington, Rio Grande, and Western Pacific over the new route after World War II, provided the Rio Grande with a measure of prosperity. The Rio Grande did manage to reduce much of its mortgage debt. In 1991 the Southern Pacific took over the much smaller Denver & Rio Grande Western.

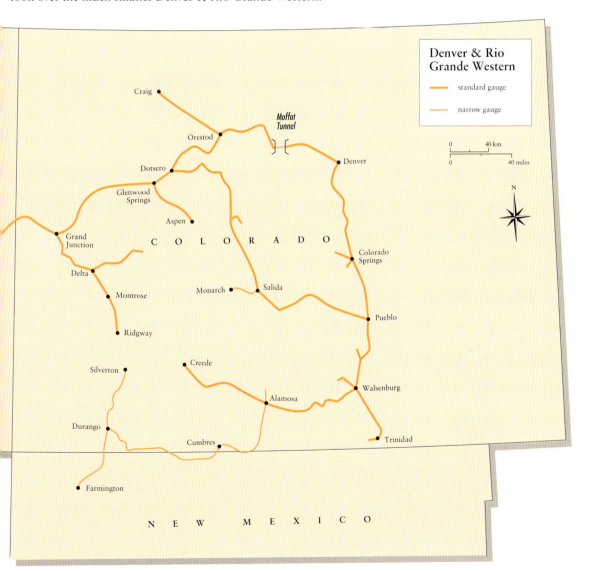

New York, Chicago & St. Louis

1950 Statistics	
(Moody's Railroads, 1951)	
Mileage	2,167
Number of states served	6
Freight revenue (millions)	$140
Passenger revenue (millions)	$2
Passenger revenue as % of freight revenue	1.4%
Total revenue (millions)	$147
Net income (millions)	$25
Operating ratio	61.1%
Employees	16,112
Workers per mile of line	7.4
Revenue per mile of line	$92,000
Locomotives	474
% diesel	17%
Freight cars	28,374
Passenger cars	111

The New York, Chicago & St. Louis Railway, known as the Nickel Plate, was conceived in 1881 by a syndicate headed by George I. Seney and Calvin S. Brice, two men known for their fast and loose financial management of several southern railroads. The line was built to serve Buffalo, Cleveland, Fort Wayne, and Chicago, and it invaded the territory dominated by Vanderbilt's Lake Short & Michigan Southern, as well as Jay Gould's Wabash Railroad. The NY,C&SL was built to such high standards that it came to be known as the "nickel-plated railroad." William H. Vanderbilt bought the line in 1883 at a high price, complaining to Calvin Brice that the line was bankrupt. Brice clinched the deal by saying, "No one knows that better than I do, but do you want to compete with a receiver?" Railroads in receivership found it easy to lower rates since such a line need not meet interest payments. In 1886 the Nickel Plate was a 523-mile road with revenue of $4 million and

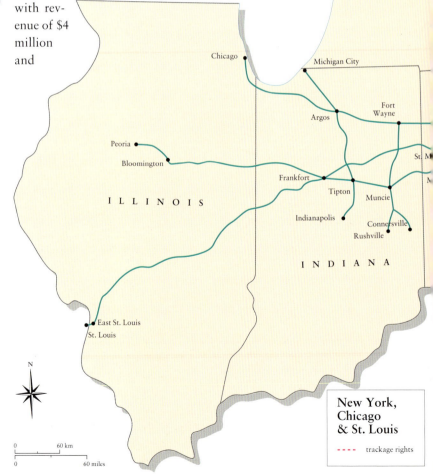

New York,
Chicago
& St. Louis

- - - - trackage rights

nearly all freight traffic.

In 1887 minority bondholders, with some help from the new ICC, forced the New York Central to give the Nickel Plate the right to be an independent operating line. For the next two or three decades the Nickel Plate was nearly moribund. In 1916 the New York Central's president, A. H. Smith, sold the Nickel Plate to the Van Sweringen brothers of Cleveland. The brothers in 1923 merged the Nickel Plate with both the Lake Erie & Western and the Toledo, St. Louis & Western to form the New York, Chicago & St. Louis Railroad (instead of Railway). The merger more than doubled the size of the Nickel Plate, with new routes in Ohio, Indiana, and Illinois. The Van Sweringens lost control of the Nickel Plate in the Great Depression.

Heavy freight traffic on the Nickel Plate duringWorld War II brought prosperity back to the line.

In the late 1940s the Delaware, Lackawanna & Western tried to buy the Nickel Plate but failed in their effort. With no commuter deficits, minimal passenger service, and fast, low-cost freight lines, the Nickel Plate by midcentury was in fine shape. The merger activity of the early 1960s made the Nickel Plate a prime target for a merger. In 1964 the Norfolk Western completed its merger with the Nickel Plate.

Midcentury Problems

American railroad mileage continued to decline in the years after World War II—from 226,696 miles in 1945 to 223,779 miles in 1950; 217,552 in 1960; and 214,387 in 1963. The second map, showing black ink spots chiefly in the western United States, shows that most Americans live within 25 miles, or half-an-hour's drive, of railroad service. The overall decline of American railroads in the last eighty years is shown in the table below.

American railroads in decline					
Year	1920	1933	1945	1965	1987
Mileage (thousands)	253	246	227	212	163
Total investment (\$billions)	20	25	24	26	47
Operating revenues (\$millions)	6,310	3,138	8,986	10,425	26,622
Railroad employees (thousands)	2,076	991	1,439	655	247
Average annual wages (current \$)	1,820	1,445	2.720	7,490	37,716
(1920 \$)	1,820	2,225	3,019	4,719	6,713
Annual freight ton-mileage per employee (thousands)	199	253	475	1,076	3,919

American railroads lost a vast amount of freight traffic to trucks between 1940 and 1960. The 3 million miles of highway and roads in the nation gave trucks a flexibility, plus door-to-door convenience that railroads could not match. In 1940 trucks moved 10 percent of the intercity freight, while railroads moved 61 percent. Because of World War II the trucks' share dropped to only 6 percent by 1945, but moved sharply up to 16 percent in 1950 and 22 percent in 1960 (44 percent for rail, 17 percent for inland waterways, and 17 percent for pipelines). Since the 1920s railroads have lost most of their less-than-carload freight plus household goods and furniture. The bulk of animals and animal products have also been lost. Between 1922 and 1960 railroad-owned refrigerator cars have dropped from 63,000 to 25,000, and railroad-owned stock cars from 80,000 to 31,000.

After V-J Day several railroads made a strong effort to revise and upgrade their passenger service. The New York Central, already having nearly three dozen name trains, in 1946 announced a \$56 million order for 710 new passenger cars. In 1952 the Pennsylvania spent \$3 million for the *New Congressional* (electric locomotive and eighteen coaches) for the New York City to Washington, D.C. run. In 1945 the Burlington had introduced the new Vista-Dome passenger equipment and in 1956 offered slumbercoaches for little more than coach fare. In the same year the Santa Fe had offered high-level passenger trains with an unobstructed view for all passengers and baggage storage and other services on the lower level. But all these innovations did little to end the drop in passenger traffic. In 1957 the commercial passenger traffic was divided: rail—31.4 percent, bus—30.7 percent, air—35.1 percent. By 1970 the figures were rail—7 percent, bus—16 percent, air—74 percent.

In the 1950s there was little letup in the federal regulation of railroads.

Railways were still subject to the same regulations of service, rates, and fares as in the days when they indeed possessed a full traffic and travel monopoly. The ICC required that railroads keep 258 types of records while airlines had to keep only a fifth as many. A railroad could not close a depot, discontinue a train, or hike a fare without requesting ICC approval. As a Boston & Maine Railroad official put it, "Every rate case has become a carnival of oratory."

The table "American railroads in decline," shown on page 116, reveals major losses in rail mileage and employment since 1920. But it also shows a great increase in the efficiency of railroad freight service since 1920. The yearly freight ton-mileage per worker has nearly doubled every fifteen years since 1920.

Of the several innovations in railroad service in the postwar years, the diesel or diesel-electric locomotive has easily been the most important. Diesels were first used in the switchyard in the 1920s and then for the new streamline passenger trains in the 1930s. As early as 1941 the Santa Fe used them for some freight service. Diesels were far more costly than steam locomotives, with most diesel units priced at $125,000 to $200,000. They were worth such prices because of their many advantages. They offered high fuel economy, low maintenance costs, and a high degree of availability. They did not require any "firing up" time, and unlike steam engines, were not thirsty for thousands of gallons

Union Pacific unit coal train loading coal in the West.

of water. Diesel units made up 10 percent of the motive power roster in 1945, 33 percent by 1950, and nearly 100 percent by 1960. By 1980 nearly all electric locomotives had also been retired. Unlike steam locomotives a single engineer could easily run two or more diesel units. Diesel unit firemen in switch and freight diesel units were reluctant to give up their "feather-bedding jobs," but were finally removed by the U.S. Supreme Court in 1964.

There were other improvements in post-war freight service. Half a dozen railroads by 1953 were offering "piggyback" service, or more correctly TOFC (trailer on flat car). By 1959 more than fifty lines had such service. A cousin of "piggyback" was COFC (container on flat car). Container freight, like piggyback, was best suited for long-haul, high-value, fast-delivery freight. The ICC for years had frowned on special train-load lower rates, but finally in 1958 permitted lower rates for unit trains hauling coal. Unit coal trains became very popular in the 1960s for moving western coal to large eastern markets.

By 1957 more than two-thirds of the nation's track was laid with rail that weighed at least 100 pounds per yard. Faster track and roadbed maintenance was possible with the ballast tampers, powered spike hammers, and other new powered track equipment. Larger cars, longer trains, and faster average speed all improved rail freight service. By 1960 the average freight-train hour produced 28,587 ton-miles of service, a figure more than twice the comparable figures for 1940.

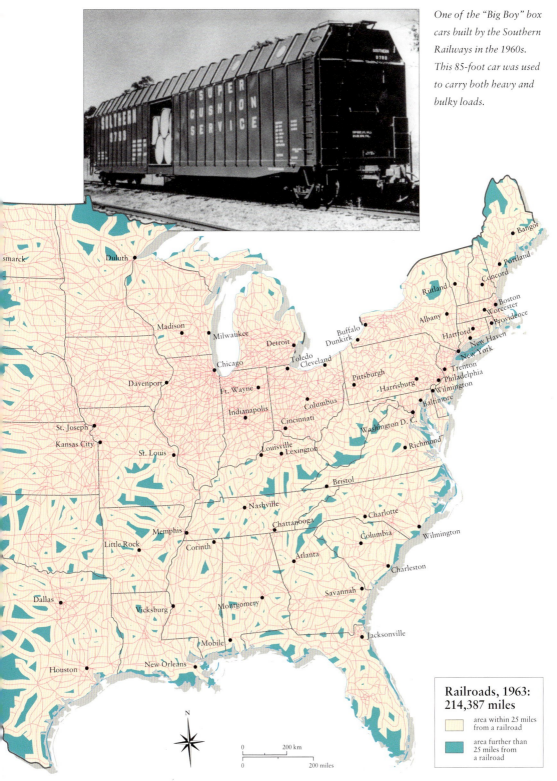

One of the "Big Boy" box cars built by the Southern Railways in the 1960s. This 85-foot car was used to carry both heavy and bulky loads.

Railroads, 1963: 214,387 miles

area within 25 miles from a railroad

area further than 25 miles from a railroad

Amtrak and Conrail, Courtesy of Uncle Sam

In 1967 John S. Reed, president of the Santa Fe, said, "Santa Fe has not abandoned the traveling public—travelers show an increasing preference to drive or fly." American railroads had lost money on their passenger service every year since 1945. Thus it was natural for them to cut passenger service when they could. In 1947 passenger trains were operating on 160,000 miles of road, a figure reduced to 112,000 miles in 1957. The Transportation Act of 1958 permitted faster passenger train discontinuances, and by 1970 the figure had dropped to 49,000 miles. Indianapolis had only eighteen daily passenger trains in 1966, less than a tenth of the 184 daily trains fifty years earlier. A few states, such as Maine, feared the loss of their last passenger trains. The general public was concerned about the growth of train discontinuance, from 20,000 passenger trains in 1929 down to only 500 in the fall of 1970.

Between 1955 and 1970 rail-freight traffic in the nation had modestly increased, while that in the Eastern District (north of the Ohio River and North Carolina and east of St. Louis and Chicago) had slightly dropped. The northeastern trunk lines were suffering from several problems: 1) the movement of many factories south or west to escape high union wages, 2) crowded and inadequate freight terminals, 3) shorter-than-average freight hauls, and 4) deficits from metropolitan commuter service. Some of these trunk lines were still paying dividends that were not justified.

Andrew J. Russell photograph of the 1869 Golden Spike ceremony. Grenville Dodge (to the right) shakes hands with Samuel Montague of the Central Pacific. Earlier Leland Stanford had aimed a husky blow at the spike, but only hit a rail.

In the same years there was considerable merger activity to the south. In 1959 the Norfolk & Western took over the Virginian Railway; in 1962 the B&O agreed to be taken over by the C&O, and in 1963 the Southern acquired the Central of Georgia. The Pennsylvania and the New York Central, longtime rivals, had been considering a merger as early as 1957. The two roads requested a merger in 1962; the ICC approved it in 1966, and the Supreme Court confirmed it in 1968. The ICC set three conditions: 1) the Penn Central would include the bankrupt New Haven, 2) the merged line must retain many redundant employees, and 3) the Pennsylvania must dispose of its Norfolk & Western stock. Stuart Saunders, the Pennsylvania president, and Alfred Perlman, the Central president, both believed the merger would save them $80 million annually.

Very little planning had preceded the 1968 merger. The giant Penn Central faced many problems. One of Saunders's aides said of the merger, "This is a big dog with a lot of fleas. . . .We'll be scratching for a long time."

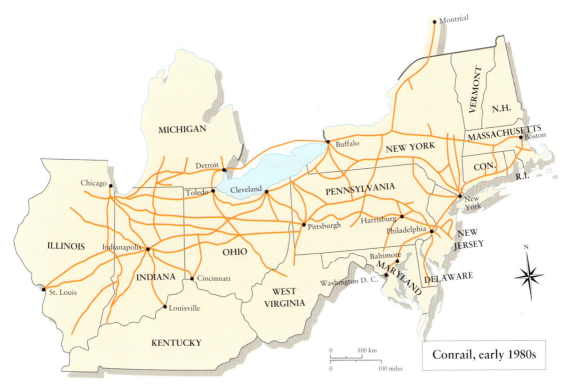

Conrail, early 1980s

The two roads were very different. One was a water-level route with gray cars and 4-6-4 *Hudsons*. The other took a shortcut via the mountains, had Tuscan red cars, and favored 4-6-2 *Pacific* steamers. The two lines used different computer and signal systems. The Central workers followed their old rules, and the Pennsylvania workers did likewise. The result was that 1968 and 1969 saw many lost waybills, lost freight shipments, and even a lost train. By 1970 the Penn Central was losing a million dollars a day. On Sunday, June 21, 1970, Penn Central filed for bankruptcy, one of the largest business failures in American history.

In the early 1970s Congress faced two major railroad problems: the collapse of passenger service and the bankruptcy of Penn Central. President Richard M. Nixon, in October 1970, signed an act creating the National Railroad Passenger Corporation that in May 1971 opened a 21,000-mile rail passenger

A modern ballast-cleaning machine in operation.

service called Amtrak. Amtrak's network stretched from Boston to San Diego and from Miami to Seattle, with 400 stations in forty-three states. Thirteen different railroads made one-time pay-ments (for a total of $190 million) to the federal government to be relieved of all passenger service. The early equipment for Amtrak—300 locomotives and

1,200 cars—was a "Rainbow Fleet" of diesel units, coaches and sleepers supplied by member railroads. Amtrak made leases for trackage rights with several railroads included in its network. The government expected that passenger ticket sales would cover from one-half to two-thirds of the Amtrak expenses. In 1972 Amtrak had revenue of $163 million and expenses of $310 million.

The Penn Central track maintenance was so poor and freight service so bad that average freight-train speed was down to 10 miles an hour. It was soon clear that there were no buyers to purchase, or bankers to reorganize, the Penn Central. Early in 1976 President Gerald Ford approved the Railroad

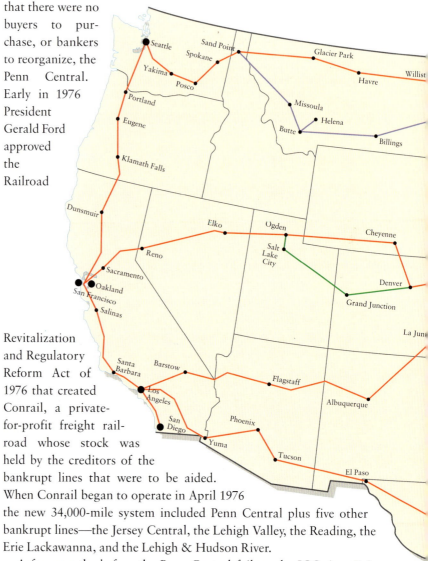

Revitalization and Regulatory Reform Act of 1976 that created Conrail, a private-for-profit freight railroad whose stock was held by the creditors of the bankrupt lines that were to be aided. When Conrail began to operate in April 1976 the new 34,000-mile system included Penn Central plus five other bankrupt lines—the Jersey Central, the Lehigh Valley, the Reading, the Erie Lackawanna, and the Lehigh & Hudson River.

A few months before the Penn Central failure the ICC, in a 7-0 vote, approved the merger of the "Hill roads"— the Burlington, the Great Northern, the Northern Pacific, and the Spokane, Portland & Seattle—into the Burlington Northern. Years of careful planning had preceded the merger. Later *Railway Age* would call the merger "the most positive development" of 1970.

Between 1960 and 1980 the cost of living roughly tripled. Inflation also hit the railroads. Average employee wages climbed from $6,270 in 1960 to $24,659 in 1980, a fourfold increase, and diesel fuel prices rose from 11¢ a gallon in 1960 to 81¢ in 1980. Freight rates rose from 1.43¢ a ton-mile in 1960 to only 2.88¢ in 1980. A decline in the workforce, longer freight cars, moving more miles a day, and the abandonment of less-used track all helped restrain the increase in freight rates.

In 1980 the nine-year old Amtrak had revenue of $454 million and expenditures of $1.08 billion for about 4 billion passenger miles of service. Between 1976 and 1980 much more than $3 billion had been spent to upgrade Conrail, and Uncle Sam's freight line was still operating very much in the red!

Amtrak
routes
from
schedule book
for July, 1971

21,000 mile passenger
network serves over 400 cities
in 43 states

●   designated end
point city

•   route identification
point

——   Amtrak route

- - -   service from
Fort Worth to
Houston to be shifted
from Temple route
to Dallas route as
soon as possible

——   added Amtrak
service

——   experimental
Amtrak route

——   non Amtrak railroad

The Staggers Rail Act of 1980

Harley O. Staggers. The Staggers Rail Act of 1980 greatly reduced the powers of the ICC.

Jimmy Carter, in the last months of his presidency, favored legislation that would, to a degree, deregulate the nation's railroads. Carter signed the Staggers Rail Act on October 14, 1980. The legislation was named for Harley O. Staggers, a West Virginia Congressman and chairman of the House Commerce Committee. The act loosened ICC regulation on mergers, abandonments, marketing, and rate making. It allowed railroads to raise rates that were below out-of-pocket costs. It also shifted the burden of proof on rate cases away from the railroad and onto the shipper. Harold H. Hall, president of the Southern Railway, said, "No longer will we have the ICC to blame for all our troubles. We will be masters of our own fate." Before long the American railroads enjoyed an increase in freight traffic, as shown in the table "U.S. Intercity Revenue Freight (1929–97)." Railroads are inclined to stress their competition with highway trucks, but this table reveals that much of the recent rail freight traffic gains since 1980 were at the expense of inland waterways and oil pipelines.

U.S. Intercity revenue freight (1929–97) ton-miles by mode (in billions)

Year	Railroads	%	Trucks	%	Waterways	%	Oil Pipelines	%	Air	%	Total
1929	455	75.0	20	3.3	106	17.5	27	4.4	0		608
1939	339	62.3	53	9.7	96	17.7	56	10.3	0		544
1944	747	68.7	58	5.3	150	13.7	133	12.2	0		1,088
1950	597	56.2	173	16.3	164	15.4	129	12.1	0		1,063
1960	579	44.1	285	21.7	220	16.7	229	17.4	1	0.1	1,314
1970	771	38.8	412	21.3	319	16.5	431	22.3	3	0.2	1,936
1980	932	37.5	555	22.3	407	16.4	588	23.6	5	0.2	2,487
1990	1,091	37.7	735	25.4	475	16.4	584	20.2	10	0.4	2,895
1993	1,183	38.1	861	27.7	456	14.7	593	19.1	12	0.4	3,105
1994	1,275	38.1	908	27.8	475	14.6	591	18.1	12	0.4	3,261
1995	1,375	40.4	921	27.0	497	14.6	601	17.6	13	0.4	3,407
1996	1,426	40.2	972	27.4	504	14.2	631	17.8	13	0.4	3,546
1997	1,421	39.2	1,051	29.0	511	14.1	628	17.3	14	0.4	3,625

On January 1, 1981, L. Stanley Crane became the top executive officer of Conrail. Conrail had abandoned some of its branch mileage since 1976. Crane was an engineer-chemist who had worked up through the technical ranks of the Southern Railway to be president by 1976. The Staggers Act allowed Crane to raise some freight rates, and the Northeast Rail Services Act of 1981 freed Conrail of its deficit-producing big-city commuter services. Crane abandoned 4,000 more miles of marginal routes, cut his average freight-train crew down to 3.1 men, and greatly increased intermodal freight, especially double-stacked container trains. By 1982 Conrail was making a small profit. In 1984 Santa Fe, CSX, and Norfolk Southern all wished to buy Conrail, but instead in 1987 it was sold to the public via the New York Stock Exchange (58 million shares at $28 a share). Crane left Conrail in 1988, and the line continued to prosper. A decade later Conrail was to be split between CSX (42 percent) and Norfolk Southern (58 percent).

L. Stanley Crane. During the 1980s, Crane rather quickly turned Conrail from red ink to dividends and private control.

The story of Amtrak in the 1980s and 1990s is not so bright. In 1980 ticket sales were paying less than half of Amtrak expenses. One of President Reagan's aides joked that it might be cheaper just to give every Amtrak passenger "a bus ticket, newspaper, and a three martini lunch." W. Graham Claytor Jr., Southern Railway president from 1967 to 1976, and secretary of the Navy in the Carter Administration, became Amtrak president in July 1982. Claytor obtained many new passenger cars for his line and lengthened working hours for train crews nearly up to a forty-hour work week. He improved the speed and service on the Metroliners so greatly that many travelers preferred Amtrak to airlines between Washington, D.C., and New York City. Claytor managed to push the revenue-to-expense ratio up to 62 percent in 1986 and even higher later. Claytor retired in 1993, and the revenue/expense ration soon declined. The Republican House of Representatives in 1995 and 1996 voted to keep Amtrak to the year 2000. When Amtrak celebrated its Silver Anniversary in 1996 few observers were willing to predict its future.

W. Graham Claytor Jr. In the 1980s Claytor greatly improved the service and reduced the expenses of Amtrak.

Many technical improvements appeared in the 1980s and 90s. Both TV and computers were increasingly used in nearly every department of the typical railroad. Centralized Traffic Control was much expanded so that some traffic centers were controlling rail traffic over several states. By the 1990s many lines were retiring most of their cabooses, replacing them with an EOTD (end-of-train-device), which protected the rear of the train with a red light and provided information to the conductor and engineer in the lead diesel unit. Such a device was reported to save 57¢ per freight-train mile. Continuous welded rail, laid down in 1,500-foot lengths, eliminated the familiar "clickety-clack" and produced maintenance savings of $1,000 per mile per year.

Railroads in the 1990s

The financial gains that many railroads hoped would accompany the Staggers Act did not appear in the early 1980s. The continuing high inflation from 1980 to 1982 made such a hope difficult. The operating revenue of Class I railroads changed very little between 1980 and 1995, averaging $28.5 billion per year in the early 1980s, $27.2 billion in the late 1980s, and $29.3 billion in the early 1990s. In the same period the average ton-mile freight rate dropped from 2.9¢ in 1980 to 2.4¢ in 1995 in current dollars. The decline in constant dollars was even greater because of inflation.

In the years after 1980 most railroads cut their operating expenses substantially. Between 1980 and 1995 many lines reduced their workforce by nearly 50 percent. During the 1980s management finally redefined a "day's work" for freight crews (set at 100 miles a day during World War I) so that it was up to 130 miles for a day's work in 1995. In 1980 total labor costs, including payroll taxes, had taken 52¢ from each revenue dollar. In 1995 the figure was only 41¢. In the same period annual fuel costs had dropped from 11.5¢ per revenue dollar to 6.5¢. Between 1980 and 1995 the average train length had increased 36 percent and the average car capacity 14 percent. Yearly loss and damage claims had dropped from $285 million to $102 million in the fifteen years.

Because of these large savings the rate of return on the stockholder's equity took a decided upturn. Between 1960 and 1979 the average rate of return was only 2.3 percent a year. In the years between 1980 and 1995 the average rate of return was 7.4 percent, and it was 9.4 percent for the four years 1992 through 1995. In 1985 the capital structure for the industry was 40 percent debt and 60 percent equity. In 1995 it was 26 percent debt and 74 percent equity.

Several mergers rather quickly followed the passage of the Staggers Act. The Burlington Northern, the CSX, the Norfolk Southern, and the Union Pacific were all active on the merger front in the early 1980s. None of these major systems, or any of the other Class I lines, retained all of their massive mileage for any length of time. Many new mergers had duplicate or parallel lines that could be leased, sold, or even abandoned. Branch lines that were unprofitable, poorly maintained routes, or routes with steep grades were also candidates for elimination. The cutbacks in route miles were sometimes drastic. The 9,500-mile Illinois Central Gulf of 1972 was down to 4,700 miles in 1985 and was only 3,000 miles by 1990. Hays Watkins reduced his CSX from 28,000 miles in 1980 to 19,000 by 1990.

Many of the lines that were dropped from new mergers as expendable or surplus still seemed essential to local shippers. These local interests often took over the abandoned or surplus line and kept the route in operation with modest subsidies from local or state governments. In 1997 there were 34 regional railroads (i.e., lines with at least 350 miles of line and/or $40 million or more of revenue), and 507 local railroads (i.e., those smaller than regional in size), in the United States. The 34 regional roads operated a total of 21,500 miles of line with 11,000 employees and $1.6 billion of annual revenue. The 507 local roads operated 28,000 miles with 12,000 workers and $1.4 billion of yearly revenue.

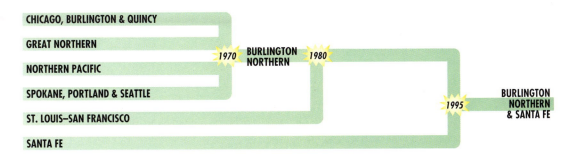

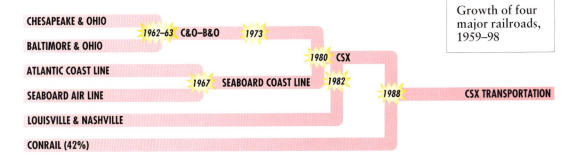

Growth of four major railroads, 1959–98

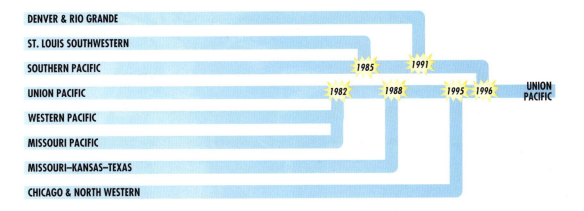

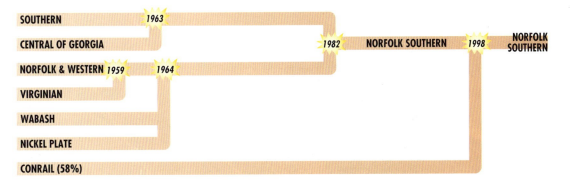

In August 1995, the Union Pacific stated its intention to purchase its rival, the 13,000-mile Southern Pacific. There was considerable opposition to the UP plan in Washington and from railroads and shippers. Before a decision was reached the Interstate Commerce Commission itself was eliminated by votes in both houses of Congress. The decision was approved by President Bill Clinton in December 1995. The ICC, the oldest regulatory agency in the nation, was replaced by a new three-member Surface Transportation Board on January 2, 1996. On July 3, 1996, the Surface Transportation Board by a 3-0 vote approved the UP-SP merger.

The ICC until 1956 defined Class I railroads as those having annual revenue of $1 million or more. Since then the ICC, and the Surface Transportation Board, have increased the revenue definition far faster than inflation: $3 million in 1956; $5 million in 1965; $50 million in 1978; and $256 million in 1997. As a

CSX double-stacked container freight trains.

result the number of Class I lines has rapidly dropped: 132 in 1939, 102 in 1963, 41 in 1978, 12 in 1988; and only 9 in 1997. The nine Class I railroads in 1997 were Union Pacific ($9.8 billion), Burlington Northern/Santa Fe ($8.4 billion), CSX ($5 billion), Norfolk Southern ($4.2 billion), Conrail ($3.6 billion), Illinois Central ($622 million), Soo ($560 million), Kansas City Southern ($516 million), and Grand Trunk Western ($352 million).

Growth and decline of railway mileage by states

State	1840	1880	1920	1965	1995
Alabama	46	1,843	5,378	4,612	3,366
Arizona	–	349	2,478	2,051	1,846
Arkansas	–	859	5,052	3,694	2,664
California	–	2,195	8,356	7,492	6,280
Colorado	–	1,570	5,519	3,760	3,439
Connecticut	102	923	1,001	734	536
Delaware	39	275	335	293	285
Florida	–	518	5,212	4,576	2,783
Georgia	185	2,459	7,326	5,565	4,518
Idaho	–	206	2,877	2,668	2,031
Illinois	–	7,851	12,188	10,956	7,663
Indiana	–	4,373	7,426	6,524	4,061
Iowa	–	5,400	9,808	8,369	4,242
Kansas	–	3,400	9,388	7,988	5,852
Kentucky	28	1,530	3,929	3,534	2,882
Louisiana	40	652	5,223	3,818	2,761
Maine	11	1,005	2,295	1,689	1,216
Maryland & (D.C.)	213	1,040	1,472	1,166	913
Massachusetts	301	1,915	2,106	1,573	949
Michigan	59	3,938	8,734	6,408	3,829
Minnesota	–	3,151	9,114	8,001	4,516
Mississippi	–	1,127	4,369	3,635	2,613
Missouri	–	3,965	8,117	6,412	4,527
Montana	–	106	5,072	4,939	3,282
Nebraska	–	1,953	6,166	5,553	3,821
Nevada	–	739	2,160	1,635	1,222
New Hampshire	53	1,015	1,252	815	320
New Jersey	186	1,684	2,352	1,845	1,047
New Mexico	–	758	2,972	2,226	2,247
New York	374	5,957	8,390	5,802	3,715
North Carolina	53	1,486	5,522	4,245	3,284
North Dakota	–	–*	5,311	5,195	3,986
Ohio	30	5,792	9,002	8,131	5,123
Oklahoma	–	289	6,572	5,570	3,434
Oregon	–	508	3,305	3,157	2,801
Pennsylvania	754	6,191	11,551	8,702	5,294
Rhode Island	50	210	211	154	100
South Carolina	137	1,427	3,814	3,261	2,361
South Dakota	–	1,225*	4,276	3,905	2,002
Tennessee	–	1,843	4,078	3,339	2,606
Texas	–	3,244	16,125	14,384	10,803
Utah	–	842	2,161	1,756	1,426
Vermont	–	914	1,077	770	569
Virginia	147	1,893	4,703	4,057	3,282
Washington	–	289	5,587	4,936	3,187
West Virginia	–	691	3,996	3,561	2,678
Wisconsin	–	3,155	7,554	6,035	3,769
Wyoming	–	512	1,931	1,848	2,065

*North and South Dakota were combined prior to 1890.

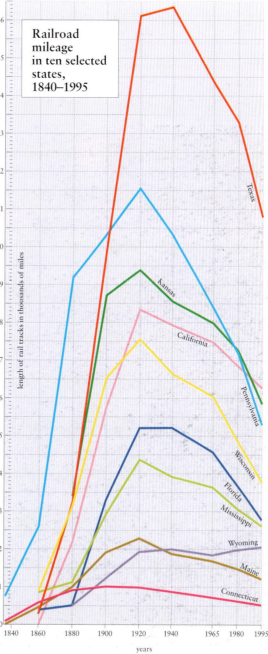

Railroad mileage in ten selected states, 1840–1995

length of rail tracks in thousands of miles

years

CHRONOLOGY

1812 Oliver Evans predicts that, before long, "carriages propelled by steam" will be in general use.

1815 Colonel John Stevens obtains from the New Jersey legislature the first railroad charter in America.

1818 Cumberland, or National, Road completed to Wheeling, Virginia.

1825 Colonel John Stevens runs his "Steam Waggon," the first operating locomotive in America, around a circular track.
Erie Canal completed.

1826 Gridley Bryant uses his broad-gauge tramway to haul granite for the Bunker Hill Monument.

1828 Charles Carroll lays the first stone for the Baltimore & Ohio Railroad, July 4.

1830 Peter Cooper's locomotive *Tom Thumb* used on the Baltimore & Ohio.
First scheduled steam railroad train service in America, by *Best Friend of Charleston*, at Charleston, South Carolina.

1831 Locomotive *DeWitt Clinton* pulls the first steam train in New York from Albany to Schenectady.
First U.S. mail carried by rail.

1833 Andrew Jackson, first president to ride on a railroad, travels between Ellicott's Mills and Baltimore, Maryland.

1835 Railroad completed to Washington, D.C., from Baltimore.

1837 American-type locomotive (4-4-0) planned and built.
First sleeping car (a crudely remodeled day coach) service.

1839 Long-distance railway express service started by William F. Harnden.

1848 *Pioneer*, Chicago's first locomotive, placed in operation.

1850 Millard Fillmore signs the first railroad land-grant act, aiding the Illinois Central and the Mobile & Ohio.

1851 Telegraph used for dispatching trains.

1852 Philadelphia and Pittsburgh linked by rail (including inclined planes).
Baltimore & Ohio completed to Wheeling on the Ohio River.

1853 All-rail route opened from the East to Chicago.

1854 Chicago and St. Louis connected by rail.
Use of coal as locomotive fuel becomes practical.

1856 Railroad bridge across Mississippi completed at Davenport, Iowa.

1857 Southern rail route from Charleston to Memphis put into operation.

1859 First Pullman sleeping car, built by George M. Pullman, makes initial run.

1860 Chicago, served by eleven railroads, becomes a major rail center.

1861–65 During the Civil War the combined freight tonnage of the Erie and the New York Central railroads for the first time exceeds that of the Erie Canal.
Abraham Lincoln signs the first Pacific Railway bill.
Experimental postal care for the sorting of mail en route put into service between Hannibal and St. Joseph, Missouri.

1863 Brotherhood of Locomotive Engineers (oldest of present railroad unions) organized.

1865 First oil tank care placed in service.
Manual block system of train control developed by Ashbel Welch.
First domestic steel rails are produced, but acceptance is slow.

1866 "Co-operative" fast-freight lines appear.

1867 Joseph G. McCoy ships first longhorns out of Abilene, Kansas, the first major cow town.
"Erie War" started, with Drew, Gould, and Fisk of the Erie opposing Commodore Vanderbilt of the New York Central.

1868 Eli H. Janney patents his automatic coupler.

1869 George Westinghouse applies for a patent for his air brake.

1871 First narrow-gauge line opened near Denver, Colorado.
Granger railroad regulation appears with legislation in Illinois and Minnesota.

1874 Windom Committee of the U.S. Senate presents a report critical of railroad abuses.
Granger legislation appears in Iowa and Wisconsin.

1877 Serious railroad labor trouble starts on the Baltimore & Ohio and spreads across the country during July.
First use of telephone communication by railroads.

1881 Steam heat for passenger equipment introduced.

1883 Standard time adopted by the railroads of the nation.

1886 Southern railroads shift from 5-foot to standard-gauge track.

1887 Interstate Commerce Act passed by Congress provides for first federal regulation of railroads.
Introduction of vestibule passenger train.
First trains fully equipped with electric lights appear.

1890 Great majority of all mileage is laid with steel rails.
1893 New York Central locomotive *No. 999* attains a speed of 112.5 miles per hour.

1894   Pullman Strike, May to July.

1895   First electrified locomotive train service in America.

1901   Mechanical coal stokers first used.

1903   Elkins Act passed by Congress attempts to strengthen the prohibition of railroad rebates.

1904   U.S. Supreme Court orders dissolution of the Northern Securities Company.

1906   Hepburn Act passed by Congress greatly increases the powers of the Interstate Commerce Commission.
All-steel passenger cars placed in regular service.

1910   Mann-Elkins Act passed by Congress further extends the jurisdiction of the ICC.
Pennsylvania Station finished in New York City.

1914   First use of radio in railroad communications.

1916   Adamson Act provides an eight-hour day for operating personnel.
Federal government provides new grants-in-aid for highway construction.

1917   National shortage of freight cars rises to 158,000 cars.
Government takes over operation of railroads on December 28.

1918   U.S. Postal Service starts air-mail service.

1920   Esch-Cummins Act, or Transportation Act of 1920, helps in the return of the railroads to private management on March 1.

1925   First diesel-electric locomotive in regular switching service.

1927   Centralized Traffic Control (CTC) has first installation.
First experiments with air-conditioned passenger cars.

1929   Greyhound bus system starts service.

1930   Air-conditioned passenger cars appear in regular service.
Rail passenger service from 1930 through 1959 operated with annual deficits except for the years 1942–45.

1934   Diesel locomotives first used in passenger service.
Introduction of lightweight streamlined passenger trains by the Burlington and the Union Pacific.

1940   Transportation Act of 1940.

1941–45 During World War II the railroads meet the transport needs of the war without government management.

1941   Diesel locomotives first used in freight service.

1945   Vista-dome passenger equipment introduced.

1952 Diesel units exceed steam locomotives.

1954 First use of television in railroad communications.
Piggyback freight service offered by several railroads.

1956 Economy slumbercoaches first used.

1957 Passenger movement by air exceeds that by rail.

1958 Transportation Act of 1958.

1960 Unit coal train operations begin.

1964 U.S. Supreme Court decides most freight train and yard firemen should be eliminated.

1965 Piggyback freight service exceeds 1 million car loadings.

1966 Pennsylvania–New York Central merger approved by ICC.

1970 Penn Central files for bankruptcy.

1971 Federal operation of Amtrak passenger service begins.

1976 Conrail begins freight service in eastern United States.

1980 Staggers Rail Act reduces ICC regulation of railroads.

1982 Conrail in the black with a small profit.

1986 Amtrak revenue reaches 62 percent of yearly expenses.
Rail management makes an agreement with labor to redefine pay scale for freight crews.

1987 Conrail common stock sold to general public.

1990 Mergers and new definition of Class I lines reduce Class I railroads to only fourteen in number.

1995 Congressional action, approved by President Clinton, eliminates ICC as a regulatory agency.
National rail network declines to 170,000 miles with 209,000 employees and only eleven Class I lines.
Rail freight service is 1,305 billion ton-miles, nearly twice the figure for 1944, the top year in World War II.

1997 Only nine Class I railroads in the nation.

FURTHER READING

General Works on Railroads

Alexander, Edwin P., *Iron Horses: American Locomotives, 1829–1900*, 1941.

Beebe, Lucius, and Charles Clegg, *Hear the Train Blow*, 1952.

Botkin, B.A., and Alvin F. Harlow (eds.), *A Treasury of Railroad Folklore*, 1953.

Bryant, Keith L., Jr., (ed.), *Railroads in the Age of Regulation, 1900–1980*, 1988.

Chandler, Alfred D., Jr., *The Railroads, The Nation's First Big Business*, 1965.

Frey, Robert L. (ed.), *Railroads in the Nineteenth Century*, 1988.

Grant, H. Roger, and Charles W. Bohi, *The Country Railroad Stations in America*, 1978.

Henry, Robert S., *This Fascinating Railroad Business*, 1942.

Hilton, George W., *American Narrow Gauge Railroads*, 1990.

Holbrook, Stewart H., *The Story of American Railroads*, 1947.

Jensen, Oliver, *The American Heritage History of Railroads in America*, 1975.

Kirkland, Edward C., *Men, Cities, and Transportation: A Study in New England History, 1820–1900*, 2 vols., 1948.

Martin, Albro, *Railroads Triumphant*, 1992

Riegel, Robert E., *The Story of Western Railroads*, 1926.

Stover, John F., *American Railroads*, 2nd ed., 1997.

Stover, John F., *The Life and Decline of the American Railroad*, 1970.

White, John H., Jr., *The American Railroad Freight Car*, 1993

White, John H., Jr., *The American Railroad Passenger Car*, 1978

White, John H., Jr., *American Locomotives, An Engineering History, 1830–1880*, 1968.

Railroad Company Histories

Athearn, Robert G., *Rebel of the Rockies*, 1962

Bryant, Keith L., Jr., *History of the Atchison, Topeka and Santa Fe Railway*, 1974.

Burgess, George H., and Miles C. Kennedy, *Centennial History of the Pennsylvania Railroad Company*, 1949.

Grant, H. Roger, *The Corn Belt Route*, 1984.

Grant, H. Roger, *Erie–Lackawanna: Death of an American Railroad, 1938–1992*, 1994

Grant, H. Roger, *The North Western*, 1996.

Harlow, Alvin F., *The Road of the Century: The Story of the New York Central*, 1947.

Hilton, George W., *Monon Route*, 1978.

Hofsommer, Don L., *The Southern Pacific, 1901–1985*, 1986.

Hungerford, Edward, *Men of Erie*, 1949.

Klein, Maury, *History of the Louisville & Nashville Railroad*, 1972.

Klein, Maury, *Union Pacific, The Birth of a Railroad, 1862–1893*, 1987.

Klein, Maury, *Union Pacific, The Rebirth, 1894–1969*, 1989.

Masterson, V. V., *The Katy Railroad and the Last Frontier*, 1952.

Overton, Richard C., *Burlington Route: A History of the Burlington Lines*, 1965.

Overton, Richard C., *Gulf to the Rockies*, 1953.

Stover, John F., *History of the Baltimore & Ohio Railroad*, 1987.

Stover, John F., *History of the Illinois Central Railroad*, 1975.

Turner, Charles W., *Chessie's Road*, 1956.

Biography

Allen, Frederick Lewis, *The Great Pierpont Morgan*, 1949.

Cochran, Thomas C., *Railroad Leaders, 1845–1890*, 1953.

Holbrook, Stewart H., *The Age of Moguls*, 1953.

Klein, Maury, *The Life and Legend of Jay Gould*, 1986.

Lane, Wheaton, J., *Commodore Vanderbilt*, 1942.

Larson, John L., *Bonds of Enterprise*, 1984.

Lewis, Oscar, *The Big Four*, 1938.

Martin, Albro, *James J. Hill and the Opening of the Northwest*, 1976.

Overton, Richard C., *Perkins / Budd*, 1982.

Perkins, J. R., *Trails, Rails and War: The Life of Grenville Dodge*, 1929.

Ward, James A., *J. Edgar Thomson*, 1980.

Ward, James A., *That Man Haupt*, 1973.

Before 1865

Black, Robert C., *The Railroads of the Confederacy*, 1952.

Fishlow, Albert, *American Railroads and the Transformation of the Ante-Bellum-Economy*, 1965.

Johnson, Arthur M., and Barry E. Supple, *Boston Capitalists and Western Railroads*, 1967.

Stover, John F., *Iron Roads to the West*, 1978.

Taylor, George R., *The Transportation Revolution, 1815–1860*, 1951.

1865–1917

Bruce, Robert V., *1877: Year of Violence*, 1959.

Lindsey, Almont, *The Pullman Strike*, 1942.

Martin, Albro, *Enterprise Denied*, 1971.

Overton, Richard C., *Burlington West*, 1941.

Stover, John F., *The Railroads of the South*, *1865–1900*, 1955.

Taylor, George R., and Irene D. Neu, *The American Railroad Network, 1861–1890*, 1956.

Ward, James A. (ed.), *Southern Railroad Man*, 1970.

Since 1917

Gray, Carl R., Jr., *Railroading in Eighteen Countries*, 1955.

Lewis, Robert G., *Handbook of American Railroads*, 1956.

McAdoo, William G., *Crowded Years*, 1931.

Miner, H. Craig, *The Rebirth of the Missouri Pacific*, 1983.

Morgan, David P., *Diesels West*, 1963.

Salsbury, Stephen, *No Way to Run a Railroad, the Untold Story of the Penn Central Crisis*, 1982.

Saunders, Richard, *The Railroad Mergers and the Coming of Conrail*, 1978.

Sharfman, I. L., *The Interstate Commerce Commission*, 4 vols., 1931–37.

Wilner, Frank N., *The Amtrak Story*, 1994.

INDEX

Adams, Charles Francis Jr., 86
Adamson Act, 54
Air Brake, 35-36, 43
Airline passenger traffic, 56, 120
Allegheny Corporation, 86
Allen, Horatio, 14
Allen, William F., 45
Alton R.R., 108
American Heritage, 88
American rail mileage and world mileage compared, 20
American Railroad Journal, 26, 28
American railroads in decline, 116–117
American Railway Association, 41
American Railway Union, 49
American type locomotive, 15
Amtrak, 121-23, 125
Anti-Trust Act of 1890, 54
Arthur, Chester A., 92
Atchison, Topeka, and Santa Fe R.R., 35, 48, 59, 90-91, 112, 124
Atlantic & Pacific R.R., 90
Atlantic & St. Lawrence R.R., 26, 40
Atlantic Coast Line 78–79, 80
Atlantic Mississippi & Ohio R.R., 84
Automatic coupler, 37, 43
Automobile age, 52, 56, 120

Baer, Roy, 59
Baldwin, Matthias, 15
Baltimore, Md., 13, 23
Baltimore & Ohio R.R., 13, 15, 16, 18, 20, 30, 31, 33, 38, 39, 43, 44, 48, 54, 60, 63, 64-65, 83, 120
Barriger, John W. III, 110
Beebe, Lucius, 64
Benton, Thomas Hart, 106
Best Friend of Charleston (locomotive), 13
Big Four Brotherhoods, 39, 54
"Black Crooks", 68
Blacklisted workers, 49
Blaine, James G., 35
Boston, Mass., 13
Boston & Worcester R.R., 16
Brice, Calvin S., 114
Bridges, 26, 42–43
Bryant, Gridley, 12
Budd, Edward G., 58
Budd, Ralph, 58–9, 60, 96
Burlington Northern R.R., 91, 93, 95, 96, 103, 122
Burlington Northern Santa Fe Corp., 91, 96, 127

Cabooses, 125
Calhoun, John C., 10
California Zephyr, 113
Camben & Amboy R.R., 13, 14
Campbell, Henry R., 15
Canadian National Ry., 77
Canals, 24
Carroll, Charles, 13
Carter, Jimmy, 124
Cascade Tunnel, 95
Casement, Daniel, 34
Casement, Jack 34
Cassatt, Alexander, J., 66
Catton, Bruce, 23
Central Pacific R.R., 34–35, 88
Centralized Traffic Control, 125
Century Progress Fair, 58, 59
Charge all the traffic will bear, 46
Charleston, S.C., 24
Charleston & Hamburg R.R., 72
Chase, Salmon P., 31
Chesapeake & Ohio Ry., 65, 82–83, 120
Chessie System, 83
Chicago, Ill., 20, 23, 38, 65
Chicago & North Western R.R., 42, 46–47, 100–01
Chicago, Burlington & Quincy R.R., 42, 46–47, 58–59, 93, 94–95
Chicago Lakefront, 26

Chicago, Milwaukee, & St. Paul R.R., 46–47, 58–59, 102-103
Chicago, Rock Island & Pacific R.R., 46–47, 87, 98–99
Chicago, St. Louis & New Orleans R.R., 76
Chicago World's Fair of 1893, 48
Cincinnati, Ohio, 22
Civil War, 23, 27, 28–31, 33, 55, 64, 76
Clark, Charles P., 105
Class I railroads, 128
Claytor, W. Graham, Jr., 73, 125
Clermont, 10
Cleveland, Cincinnati, St. Louis & Chicago R.R., 69
Clinton, Bill, 128
Clinton, Dewitt, 10
Clyde, W.P., 72
"Coal Roads", 62
Coffin, Lorenzo S., 43
Colfax, Schuyler, 35
Colorado & Southern R.R., 96
Common carriers, 15
Competition for the railroad since 1900, 56–57
Confederate railroads, 28–29
Congress adopts standard time, 45
Connestoga wagon, 10
Conrail, 121–122, 125
Container freight trains, 118, 128
Continental railway system, 54
Cooke, Jay, 35, 38, 92
Corning, Erastus, 16, 68
Cost per mile in building railroads, 17, 21
Council for National Defense, 54, 60
Crane, L. Stanley, 125
Credit Mobilier, 34–35, 86, 92
Crocker, Charles, 34, 88
CSX, 65, 74, 78, 80, 83, 125, 127, 128

Debs, Eugene V., 49
De Butts, Harry A., 73
Delaware, Lackawanna & Western R.R., 125
Democratic Party, 33
Denver & Rio Grande R.R., 42, 89, 90, 112–113
Denver Pacific R.R., 35
Denver to Chidago Zephyr trip, 58–59
Denver Zephyr, 96
Depots, 88, 104
Depression of 1930s, 60, 115
Dewitt Clinton (locomotive), 13
Diesel locomotives, 58–59, 65, 117–118
Dining car service, 36, 63
Diplomatic travel time, 10
Dodge, Grenville M.,34, 120
Douglas, Stephen A., 32, 108
Dowd, C.F., 45
Drew, Daniel, 70
Durant, Thomas C., 34

Eads, James B., 42
Earling, Albert J., 102
Eastman Joseph B., 60
Eaton, Cyrus., 53
Effie Afton (steamboat), 98
Eight-hour day, 54
Election of 1860, 18–19
Electric interurban lines, 57
Electric locomotives, 49, 66, 103, 104
Elkins Act, 51
Employees, 38, 39, 43, 48–49, 53, 55, 60–61, 62, 116, 123, 126
English trains, 24
Ennis, George, 16
Erie Canal, 10, 12, 14, 36, 64
Erie R.R., 20, 22, 36, 40, 48, 70–71
Erie–Lackawanna R.R., 71
Evans, Oliver, 12
Experiment (locomotive), 14
Extent of rail mileage, 20

Fairlie, Robert F., 42
Farnam, Henry, 98

Farrington, John D., 98
Fast freight lines, 36
Fast passenger trains, 49, 69
Featherbedding jobs, 118, 126
Featherstonhaugh George W., 13
Federal Highway program of 1916, 52
Federal operations of railroads, 55, 60
Federal rail regulations, 117
Female railroad workers (WW II), 60, 61
Fillmore, Millard, 32, 70
Fink, Albert, 74
Fish, Stuyvesant, 42–43
Fisk, Jim, 39, 70
Florida, Central and Penninsular R.R., 80
"Flying Machine", 10
Forbes, John Murray, 96
Ford, Gerald, 122
Fraser, Donald V., 110
Free passes, 46
Freight cars, 15, 60
Freight rates, 22, 38, 39, 49, 53, 54, 123, 124, 125, 126
Freight revenue, 62, 116, 120, 124
Freight ton-mileage (per year per worker) 53, 116
Frontier line (1865), 34
Fuel costs, 123, 126
Fulton, Robert, 10
Funded debt, 61

Galena & Chicago Union R.R., 100
Gallatin, Albert, 10
Garfield, James A., 35
Garrett, John W., 31, 38, 39, 64
Gauge: standard, 14, 26, 40–41, variety of, 14, 26–27; southern, 14, 26
General Time Convention, 45
Georgia and Alabama R.R., 80
Giant windmill, 34
Golden Age of American Railroads, 52,55
Golden Spike Ceremony, 34, 86, 120
Gould, George, 50, 106, 112–113
Gould, Jay, 50, 70, 106, 110, 112, 114
Gould system, 50–51
Grain elevator abuses, 46
Granger laws, 46
Granger railroads, 46–47
Grant, Ulysses S., 33, 76, 92
"Great American West", 34
Great Northern Ry., 35, 94–95, 96
"Great Western Mail", 18
Greely Horace, 25, 34
Green Diamond, 59
Gulf, Mobile & Ohio R.R., 77, 108–109
Guthrie, James, 28, 74

Hale, Nathan, 16
Hall, Harold H., 124
Hand brakes, 43
Hannibal and St. Joseph R.R., 36, 96
Harriman, Edward H., 43, 50, 52, 76, 86, 89, 94, 96
Harriman Roads, 50, 51
Harrison, Fairfax, 93
Harvey, Frederick H., 90
Heinman, Ben W., 101
Hepburn Act, 51
Hill, James J., 35, 50, 94–95, 96
Hill Roads, 50–51, 52, 93
Holliday, Cyrus K., 90
Hopkins, Mark, 34, 88
Hughett, Marvin, 100
Huntington, Collis P., 34, 52, 82, 86, 88

Illinois, 32
Illinois Central R.R., 20, 32–33, 41, 42, 59, 76–7, 108
Illinois Central Gulf R.R., 77
Increased operating efficiency, 53, 60, 116
Indian Territory, 110
Inflation, 28, 53, 123, 126
Ingalls, Melville E., 82
Interchange of freight cars, 27, 42

Intercity bus traffic, 56
Intercity truck traffic, 56–57, 116, 124
Internal combustion engine, 56
Interstate Commerce Act of 1887, 47
Interstate Commerce Commission, 48, 91, 98, 117, 120, 124, 128
Investment in railroads, 16, 53, 116, 128
"Iowa Pool", 46

Janney, Eli H., 37, 43
Jenks, Downing B., 107
Jervis, John B., 14
Jewitt, Hugh, 40
Johnston, Wayne, 77

Kansas Pacific R.R., 35, 112
Kelley, Oliver H., 46
Kettering, Charles F., 58
Kilbourn, Byron, 102
Kimball, Frederick J., 84
King, William R., 32, 108
Kruttschnitt, Julius, 89

Lake Shore & Michigan Southern R.R., 69, 114
Land grants (Federal), 20, 32–33, 61, 86, 92, 96
Lend Lease Act, 60
Less-than-car-load lot freight, 57
Life on the Mississippi, 23
Lincoln, Abraham, 17–18, 31, 34, 98
"Link-and-pin" coupler, 37, 43
Locomotives, 14, 20, 23, 31, 33, 42–43, 49, 56, 58–59, 67, 69, 101, 108
Loder, Benjamin, 16, 26, 70
Long-and-short-haul abuses, 46
Longstreet, James, 31
Lord, Eleazor, 70
Louisville & Nashville R.R., 28, 41, 74–75, 80
Lovett, Robert S., 86

M-10000 streamliner, 59
McAdoo, William G., 76
McComb, Henry S., 76
McKeen Motor Cars, 59
Mahone William, 84
"Main Line of Mid-America", 76
Main Line of Pennsylvania, 12, 66
Major Rail Combinations in early 20th century, 50–51
Major troop movements in the Civil War, 30–31
Mann-Elkins Act, 51
Mason, William, 20
Meals on passenger trains, 25, 36
Mellen, Charles S., 105
Mergers, 120, 121, 124, 126, 128
Metroliners, 125
Michigan Central R.R., 69
Mileage, 13, 15, 16, 17, 21, 28, 36, 37, 38, 40, 41, 48, 50–51, 52, 53, 60, 62, 116, 119, 123
Milwaukee & Mississippi R.R., 102
Minnesota & Pacific R.R., 94
Missouri River, 34
Missouri, Kansas & Texas R.R., 84, 110–11
Missouri Pacific R.R., 87, 106–07, 110
Mississippi (locomotive), 108
Mississippi & Missouri R.R., 98
Mitchell, Alexander, 102
Mobile & Ohio R.R , 32, 41, 108
Model T. Ford, 56
Moffat Tunnel, 113
Mohawk & Hudson R.R., 13, 16
Moore, William H., 50
Morgan, J.P., 50–51, 52, 72, 105
Morgan Roads, 50–51
"Mother of Railroads", 64

Narrow gauge railroads, 42
Nashville, Chattanooga & St. Louis R.R. 74
National Grange, 46–47
National, or Cumberland Road, 10, 18
Nevins, Allan, 26
Newcomer, Benjamin R., 78
New Orleans, La., 10, 22–23, 24

New Western States, 12
New York & Harlem R.R., 37, 68
New York Central R.R., 16, 22, 24, 28, 31, 36, 39, 49, 68–69, 115
New York, Chicago & St. Louis Ry., 85, 114–115
New York City, 12, 23, 24
New York, New Haven, & Hartford R.R., 104–105, 120
Nixon, Richard M., 121
No. 999 (locomotive), 49, 69
Norfolk & Petersburg R.R., 84
Norfolk & Western R.R., 73, 84–85, 115, 120
Norfolk & Southern R.R., 73, 85, 125, 127
Northern Central R.R., 29
Northern Pacific R.R., 35, 48, 92–93, 96
Northern Securities Co., 95

Official Guide of the Railways, 45
Ogden, William Butler, 100
Ohio & Mississippi R.R., 22, 40
Oil pipelines, 124
"Old Reliable", 74
Olney, Richard S., 48, 51
Operating ratio, 61, 62
Operating revenue, 53, 62, 116
Opposition to railroads, 14
Opposition to standard time, 45
Oregon Short Line, 35
Osborn, William, 76

Pacific (locomotive), 106
Pacific Railway Bill, 34
Palmer, William Jackson, 42 112
Panic of 1837, 14
Panic of 1873, 35, 38, 88, 92
Panic of 1893, 48, 86
Parsons, Levi, 110
Passenger cars, 15, 24
Passenger traffic, 56, 58, 62, 86, 116, 120
Passenger train discontinuance, 120–21
Paxson, Frederick, 46
Penn Central, 67, 69, 105, 120–21
Pennsylvania R.R., 16, 20, 22, 31, 36, 39, 41, 65, 66–67, 81, 122
Pennsylvania Group, 50–51
Per diem charge, 42
Pere Marquette R.R., 83
Perham, Josiah, 92
Perkins, Charles E., 96
Perlman, Alfred, 120
Petersburg R.R., 28
Philadelphia, Pa., 23, 26
Piedmont R.R., 30
Piggy-back service, 118
Pioneer Zephyr (streamliner), 58–59
Pittsburgh, Pa., 10, 22, 39
Plant, Henry Bradley, 78
Pocahontas coal field, 85
Poor, John A., 26
Progressive Movement, 51, 56
Promontory Point, 35
Pullman, George, 24
Pullman Palace Car Co., 49
Pullman Strike, 48–49, 100

Railroad accidents, 104
Railroad Gazette, 45
Railroad passenger miles, 56
Railroad passenger schedules, 24
Railroad receivership, 35, 48, 114
Railroad revenues, 53, 62, 116, 126
Railroad strikes, 39, 48–49, 65
Railroad unions, 39, 49
Railroads, a big complex business, 20
Railroads of the Northeast, 16, 21, 120
Railroads of the Old Northwest and Midwest, 16, 21
Railroads of the South, 16, 21
"Rainbow Fleet", 121–22
Rails, 14, 29–30, 118, 125
Railway Age, 122
Raleigh & Gaston R.R., 80

Rate of return for stockholders, 126
Rate wars, 34–39, 65
Raton Pass, 90, 112
Reading R.R., 48
Reagan, Ronald, 125
Rebates, 46
Reconstruction Finance Co., 77
Reed, John S., 120
Regional and local railroads, 126
Reid-Moore Syndicate, 98
Republican Party, 23
Richmond, Va., 26
Richmond & Danville R.R., 29, 30, 48, 72
Ripley, Edward P., 91
Roadbed, 14, 70
Robinson, John M., 80
Rock Island Bridge, 98
Rock Island System, 50–51
Roosevelt, Franklin D., 60
Roosevelt, Theodore, 51

St. Louis, Iron Mountain & Southern R.R., 106
St. Louis, Mo., 20–22
St. Paul & Pacific R.R., 94
St. Paul, Minneapolis & Manitoba Ry., 94
Sale of land grant acres, 46
Saratoga, N.Y., 39
Saunders, Stuart, 120–21
"Scarlet Woman" of Wall St., 70
Schiff, Jacob H., 86
Schuyler, Robert, 104
Scott, Tom, 31, 39, 66, 72
Seaboard Air Line, 78, 80–81
Seaboard & Roanoke R.R., 80
Seaboard Coast Line, 74, 78, 80
Seney, George I., 114
Sherman, William T., 55
Sleeping cars, 24, 116
Slumber coach, 116
Smith, A.H., 115
Smith, Milton H., 41, 74
"Snakeheads", 14
South Carolina Canal and Railroad Co., 13
Southern Pacific R.R., 35, 86, 88–89, 91, 113, 128
Southern Ry., 48, 72–73, 108
Speed of travel: in 1800, 10; in 1860, 24–25
Spencer, Samuel, 72–73
Spokane, Portland, & Seattle R.R., 93, 96
Springfield, Ill., 18
Stagecoach travel, 12, 18
Staggers, Harley O., 124
Staggers Rail Act of 1980, 124, 126
Standard gauge achieved, 40–41
"Standard" railroad of the country, 66
Standard Time, 44, 45
Stanford, Leland, 34, 88
Stanton, Edwin M., 31
State aid in building railroads, 17
Steamboat traffic, 10, 18, 22–23
Stephenson, George, 12
Stevens, John, 12, 13
Stevens, Robert, 14
Stockton & Darlington Ry., 12
Streamliners, 58–59
Strong, William B., 35, 90
Super Chief, 59, 91
Surface Transportation Board, 128

Taft, William Howard, 51
Tank cars, 36
Taylor, Zachary 18
Telegraphic train control, 20, 71
Thomas, Philip E., 13, 14
Thompson, John Edgar, 16, 66
Tigrett, Isaac B., 108
"Time ball", 44
Time zones, 45
Track, 14
Trade and commerce of Old Northwest shifts from river steamboat to the railroads in the 1850s, 22–3
Traffic on Ohio and Mississippi Rivers, 22–23

Transcontinental lines, 34–35, 62
Transportation Act of 1920, 55
Transportation Act of 1958, 120
Tredegar Iron Works, 30
Trunk lines, 16, 39, 62
Tuohy, Walter J., 83
Turnpikes, 10
Twentieth Century, 65
Two Roads to Sumter, 23

Underwood, Frederick, 71
Union Pacific R.R., 34–35, 44, 48, 59, 86, 98, 101,
    107, 110, 127, 128
Union Pacific Southern Branch R.R., 110
Unit coal train, 117–118
U.S. Army engineers, 32
U.S. mail and railroads, 36
U.S. military railroads, 30
U.S. Supreme Court, 47, 54, 86, 90, 96, 112, 120
Utica & Schenectady, R.R., 16, 68

Vanderbilt, Cornelius, 37, 39, 43, 44, 50, 68–69,
    70
Vanderbilt, William, H., 69, 114
Vanderbilt Roads, 50–51
Van Sweringen, Mantis J., 82 106, 115
Van Sweringen, Otis P., 82, 106, 115
Vestibule passenger cars, 43
Villard, Henry, 92
Vista-Dome passenger cars, 96
Virginia Central R.R., 82
Virginia Ry., 85

Wabash R.R., 114
Wages, railroad, 53, 55, 62, 116, 123
Wagon freight rates, 10
Walters, Henry, 78
Walters, William T., 78
Washington, D.C., 13, 18–19
Water way traffic, 124
Watkins, Hays T., 82–83, 126
"Web of Transport" (1850s), 26
Webster, Daniel, 70
Weldon & Raleigh R.R., 80
Western Canals, 22
Western Maryland R.R., 83
Western Pacific R.R., 87. 91
Westinghouse, George, 36, 37, 43
Wickham, William C., 82
Willard, Daniel, 54, 64, 65
William Galloway (locomotive), 14
William Mason (locomotive), 20
Wilmington & Manchester R.R., 78
Wilmington & Weldon R.R., 78
Wilson, Woodrow, 54, 55
Winans, Ross, 33
Workers per mile of railroad in 1950, 62
World War I, 54–55, 56, 61
World War II, 60–61, 62
Wrecked locomotive, 31

Young, Robert R., 82–83

Zephyrs, 96

MAP PLACE NAME INDEX

Aberdeen, 77, 101, 103
Abilene, 35
Akron, 65, 67, 71
Alabama, 15, 17, 21, 22, 25, 27, 29, 32, 33, 45, 51,
    73, 75, 77, 79, 81, 109
Alamosa, 113
Alazon, 89
Albany, 11, 13, 15, 17, 19, 21, 23, 27, 49, 53, 57,
    61, 69, 79, 81, 119, 123
Albert Lea, 47, 77
Albuquerque, 35, 91, 122
Alexandria, 73, 83, 89, 107
Alliance, 97
Altoona, 67, 122-123

Altus, 111
Amarillo, 91, 97, 99
Americus, 81
Antron, 77
Arcadia, 115
Argos, 115
Arizona, 33, 35, 89, 91
Arizona Territory, 28, 32, 44, 51
Arkansas, 15, 17, 21, 22, 25, 27, 29, 32, 33, 35, 44,
    51, 75, 89, 99, 107, 109
Artesia, 109
Ash Fork, 91
Asheville, 73, 123
Ashland, 83, 93, 101
Ashtabula, 67, 115
Aspen, 113
Atchison, 35, 91, 107
Athens, 17, 75, 83
Atlanta, 15, 17, 21, 27, 29, 37, 39, 41, 49, 53, 57,
    61, 73, 75, 79, 81, 119, 123
Atlantic, 99
Atlantic City, 67
Augusta, 73, 79, 123
Aurora, 97
Austin, 89, 103, 107, 111

Bainville, 94-95
Bakersfield, 91
Baldwin, 81, 83
Baltimore, 13, 15, 17, 19, 21, 23, 27, 37, 39, 41, 49,
    53, 57, 61, 65, 67, 119, 123, 121
Bangor, 15, 17, 19, 21, 27, 49, 53, 57, 61, 119
Barstow, 86, 91, 122
Baton Rouge, 77, 107
Battle Creek, 123
Bay City, 69, 83
Bay Head, 67
Bay St. Louis, 75
Beacon, 104
Beatrice, 47
Beaumont, 89, 91
Beckley, 83
Bedford, 103
Belen, 91
Bell, 81
Belleville, 47
Bellevue, 115
Beloit, 103
Bend, 86, 92, 94
Benid, 101
Benton Harbor, 83
Bessemer, 81
Bieber, 94-95
Billings, 92, 94, 97, 122
Binghamton, 71
Birmingham, 73, 75, 77, 79, 81, 109, 123
Bismarck, 35, 39, 41, 49, 53, 57, 61, 107, 119, 123
Bloomington, 77, 109, 115
Blue Ridge, 75
Bluefield, 84-85
Bogalusa, 109
Boise, 86-87
Boone, 102-103
Boston, 11, 13, 15, 17, 19, 21, 25, 27, 37, 39, 41,
    49, 53, 57, 61, 69, 105, 119, 121, 123
Bowie, 47
Bowling Green, 75
Bozeman, 102
Bradford, 71
Brady, 91
Brewster, 47, 115
Bristol, 21, 27, 49, 53, 57, 61, 73, 84, 119
Brookfield, 97
Brookhaven, 77
Brownsville, 69, 89, 107
Brunswick, 73
Bucklin, 47
Buffalo, 15, 17, 19, 21, 23, 27, 37, 39, 41, 49, 53,
    57, 61, 65, 69, 71, 83, 115, 119, 121, 123
Buffalo Gap, 47
Burkeville, 85
Burlington, 59, 97, 99

Butka, 47
Butte, 86, 92, 94, 102, 122

Cadiz, 91
Cairo, 15, 19, 22, 69, 77, 123
Caliente, 86-87
California, 21, 27, 28, 32, 33, 35, 44, 51, 86, 89,
    91, 94
Camden, 99
Cameron, 47
Canada, 69, 83
Canon City, 91
Canton, 115, 123
Canyon, 91
Cape Charles, 67
Cape May, 67
Carbondale, 77
Casper, 101
Cedar Rapids, 77, 99, 103
Centralia, 77
Chadron, 101
Chamberlain, 47
Champaign, 77
Champion, 103
Channing, 103
Charleston, 11, 13, 15, 17, 21, 27, 29, 37, 39, 41,
    49, 53, 57, 61, 65, 69, 73, 79, 81, 83, 119, 123
Charlotte, 15, 21, 27, 29, 37, 39, 41, 49, 53, 57, 61,
    73, 81, 119, 123
Charlottesville, 73, 83, 123
Chatham, 69
Chattahoochee, 81, 75
Chattanooga, 15, 17, 21, 27, 29, 37, 39, 41, 49, 53,
    57, 61, 73, 75, 119
Cherokee, 77
Cheyenne, 35, 47, 87, 97, 122
Chicago, 15, 17, 19, 21, 23, 25, 27, 35, 37, 39, 41,
    47, 49, 53, 57, 59, 61, 65, 67, 69, 71, 77, 83, 89,
    91, 97, 99, 101, 103, 109, 115, 119, 121, 123
Chillicothe, 84
Cincinnati, 15, 17, 19, 21, 22, 23, 27, 37, 39, 41,
    49, 53, 57, 61, 65, 67, 69, 71, 73, 75, 83, 84,
    119, 121, 123
Clarksdale, 77
Clarksville, 75
Clear Lake, 99
Cleburne, 91
Cleveland, 15, 17, 19, 21, 25, 27, 37, 39, 41, 49,
    53, 57, 61, 65, 67, 69, 71, 115, 119, 121, 123
Clinton, 77, 99, 101
Clovis, 91
Cody, 97
Coffeyville, 91, 107
Colby, 86-87
Colfax, 94
Colorado, 35, 32, 33, 44, 47, 51, 59, 87, 89, 91, 97,
    99, 107, 113
Colorado Springs, 47, 99, 113
Colorado Territory, 28
Columbia, 15, 17, 21, 27, 37, 39, 41, 49, 53, 57,
    61, 73, 75, 77, 81, 119, 123
Columbus, 15, 17, 19, 21, 27, 29, 37, 39, 41, 47,
    49, 53, 57, 61, 65, 67, 69, 73, 81, 83, 84, 119,
    123
Concord, 15, 17, 21, 27, 49, 53, 57, 61, 119
Concordia, 47
Connecticut, 11, 13, 15, 17, 19, 21, 22, 25, 27, 29,
    32, 33, 45, 51, 69, 104, 121
Connellsville, 65, 69
Connersville, 115
Corbin, 75
Corinth, 21, 27, 37, 39, 41, 49, 53, 57, 61, 109, 119
Corpus Christi, 89, 107
Corsicana, 89
Council Bluffs, 77, 87, 101
Covington, 77
Craig, 113
Creede, 113
Crestline, 67
Crestview, 75
Crossett, 99
Cumberland, 17, 19, 65, 67

Cumbres, 113
Dakota Jc., 47
Dakota Territory, 27, 28-9, 32, 44
Dalhart, 99
Dallas, 39, 41, 49, 53, 57, 61, 89, 91, 97, 99, 107, 111, 119, 123
Danbury, 104
Danville, 69, 73
Davenport, 15, 21, 27, 37, 39, 41, 49, 53, 57, 61, 103, 119
Dawson, 89
Dayton, 65, 67, 71, 123
Deadwood, 47
Decatur, 17, 77
Decorah, 47, 99
Del Rio, 123
Delaware, 11, 13, 15, 17, 19, 21, 22, 23, 25, 27, 29, 32, 33, 45, 51, 65, 67, 69, 73, 83, 121
Delta, 113
Deming, 91
Denison, 111
Denver, 35, 39, 41, 47, 49, 53, 57, 59, 61, 87, 91, 97, 99, 113, 118, 122
Des Moines, 47, 97, 99, 101, 103
Deshler, 65
Detroit, 15, 17, 19, 21, 27, 37, 39, 41, 49, 53, 57, 61, 67, 69, 83, 115, 119, 121, 123
Devils Lake, 95
Dixon, 77
Dodge City, 35, 47, 91, 99, 123
Dotsero, 113
Dover, 67
Du Guoin, 77
Dubuque, 77
Duluth, 35, 39, 41, 47, 49, 53, 57, 61, 93, 95, 101, 103, 119
Dunkirk, 21, 27, 49, 53, 57, 61, 71, 119
Dunsmuir, 122
Durango, 113
Durbin, 83
Durham, 81, 85
Dyersburg, 77

East St. Louis, 109, 115
Eau Claire, 47
Edgeley, 102-103
Effingham, 77, 123
Effner, 67
Egan, 102-103
El Dorado, 99
El Paso, 35, 39, 41, 49, 53, 57, 61, 89, 91, 107, 118, 123
El Reno, 99
Elkhorn City, 83
Elko, 122
Ellsworth, 47
Elmira, 67, 71
Emporia, 123
Englewood, 91
Enid, 99
Ephraim, 113
Erie, 67, 71, 115
Etowah, 75
Eugene, 89, 92, 122
Eunice, 99
Eureka, 89, 113
Evansville, 69, 73, 75, 77, 101
Everett, 102

Fairport, 65
Fargo, 47, 93, 95, 103, -123
Farmington, 113
Fiomaton, 75
Fitchburg, 105
Flagstaff, 122
Fleming, 75
Flint, 83
Florence, 79
Florida, 17, 21, 22, 25, 27, 29, 32, 33, 45, 51, 73, 75, 79, 81
Florida Territory, 13, 15
Floydada, 91

Fort Dodge, 77
Fort Madison, 91
Fort Smith, 107
Fort Wayne, 15, 21, 27, 23, 49, 53, 57, 61, 67, 69, 115, 119, 123
Fort Worth, 89, 91, 97, 99, 107, 111, 123
Fostoria, 83
Frankfort, 17, 83, 115
Franklin City, 67
Frederick, 67
Freeport, 77
French Louisiana, 11
Fresno, 91
Fulton, 77

Galax, 84
Gale, 107
Galesburg, 91
Galion, 69
Galveston, 89, 97, 99, 107, 111
Garden City, 91
Gasper, 47
Georgia, 11, 13, 15, 17, 21, 22, 25, 27, 29, 32, 33, 45, 51, 73, 75, 79, 81
Georgiana, 75
Gettysburg, 47
Glacier Park, 123
Glade Spring, 84
Glenwood Springs, 113
Godsden, 75
Goldsboro, 17, 73
Goodland, 47
Graceville, 75
Grafton, 65
Grand Canyon, 91
Grand Forks, 93,-95, 123
Grand Island, 87
Grand Junction, 113, 122
Grand Rapids, 69, 83
Great Falls, 94, 102
Great Northern, 35
Green Bay, 101, 103
Green River, 86
Greensboro, 73
Greenville, 77, 123
Greenwood, 77, 81
Gulfport, 75, 77
Guthrie, 75

Hagerstown, 85
Hamlet, 81, 123
Hammond, 71, 77
Harlan, 75
Harlowton, 103
Harrington, 47
Harrisburg, 15, 17, 19, 21, 27, 49, 53, 57, 61, 67, 119, 121, 123
Harrisonburg, 73
Hartford, 17, 21, 27, 49, 53, 57, 61, 105, 119, 123
Hattiesburg, 77
Havre, 94-95, 122
Helena, 39, 41, 49, 52, 56, 60, 77, 92, 107, 118, 122
Helper, 113
Henderson, 81
Herington, 47, 99
Hickory, 73
High Springs, 79
Hillsboro, 84
Hodgeville, 77
Hoisington, 107
Holland, 83
Hoover Dam, 86
Hopkinsville, 77
Hoquiam, 86
Hornell, 71
Horton, 47
Hot Springs, 99
Houghton, 47
Houston, 21, 27, 37, 39, 41, 49, 52-53, 57, 61, 89, 91, 97, 99, 107, 111, 119, 123
Huntington, 71, 83

Hutchinson, 91
Hyannis, 105

Idaho, 33, 35, 51, 86, 92, 94, 102
Idaho Territory, 28, 32, 44
Illinois, 15, 17, 19, 21, 22, 23, 25, 27, 29, 32, 33, 35, 45, 47, 51, 59, 65, 67, 69, 71, 73, 75, 77, 83, 89, 91, 97, 99, 101, 103, 107, 109, 115, 121
Indian Territory, 27, 29
Indiana, 15, 17, 19, 21, 23, 22, 25, 27, 29, 32, 33, 45, 51, 65, 67, 69, 71, 73, 75, 77, 83, 103, 115, 121
Indiana Territory, 11
Indianapolis, 15, 17, 19, 21, 27, 29, 37, 39, 41, 49, 53, 57, 61, 65, 67, 69, 71, 77, 115, 119, 121, 123
International Falls, 93
Iowa, 17, 19, 21, 22, 25, 27, 29, 32, 33, 35, 45, 47, 51, 59, 77, 87, 89, 95, 97, 99, 101, 103
Iowa Falls, 99
Iowa Territory, 15
Ishpeming, 101

Jackson, 17, 69, 75, 77, 109, 123
Jacksonville, 21, 27, 37, 39, 41, 49, 53, 57, 61, 73, 79, 81, 119, 123
Jamestown, 71
Jefferson City, 107, 111, 123
Jenkins, 83
Johnstown, 65
Joliet, 103, 109
Joplin, 91, 111

Kalamazoo, 123
Kankakee, 77
Kansas, 27, 29, 32, 33, 35, 45, 47, 51, 59, 87, 89, 91, 97, 99, 103, 107, 111
Kansas City, 35, 39, 41, 47, 49, 53, 57, 61, 87, 89, 91, 97, 99, 103, 107, 109, 111, 119, 123
Kansas Territory, 21, 25, 27
Kearny Jc., 47
Keeler, 89
Kenova, 84-85
Kentucky, 11, 15, 17, 19, 21, 22, 25, 27, 29, 32, 33, 45, 51, 65, 67, 73, 75, 77, 83, 85, 109, 121
Keokuk, 47, 99
Ketchum, 87
Kewaunee, 83
Keyes, 111
Kinder, 107
Klamath Falls, 89, 122
Knoxville, 73, 75

La Crosse, 15, 47, 83, 103
La Junta, 91, 122
La Salle, 77
Lafayette, 123
Lake Charles, 107
Lake Erie, 83
Lake Huron, 83
Lake Michigan, 83
Lake Ontario, 83
Lamy, 91
Lancaster Pike, 11
Lander, 101
Lansing, 83
Laramie, 87
Laredo, 107
Larned, 107
Las Vegas, 86
Latonia, 75
Laurel, 77, 92, 94
Laws, 89
Leadville, 97
Lewiston, 81, 86
Lexington, 15, 17, 21, 27, 49, 53, 57, 61, 65, 73, 83, 119
Liberal, 47, 99
Lima, 67, 71, 123
Limon, 47, 99
Lincoln, 59, 77, 86-87, 97, 99, 101, 107, 123
Little Rock, 21, 27, 37, 39, 41, 49, 53, 57, 61, 99, 107, 119

Logan, 83
Logansport, 67
Long Island, 104
Longview, 91, 102, 107
Lorain, 65
Los Angeles, 35, 39, 41, 49, 53, 57, 61, 87, 89, 91, 119, 123
Louisiana, 15, 17, 21, 22, 25, 27, 29, 32, 33, 35, 45, 51, 73, 75, 77, 89, 91, 99, 107, 109
Louisville, 15, 17, 19, 21, 27, 29, 49, 53, 57, 61, 65, 67, 73, 75, 77, 83, 119, 121, 123
Lowell, 105
Lubbock, 91
Lynchburg, 73, 83, 85
Lynndyl, 86

Mackinaw City, 67, 69
Macon, 73, 81
Madison, 15, 17, 21, 27, 49, 53, 57, 61, 67, 77, 101, 103, 119
Maine, 13, 15, 17, 19, 21, 22, 25, 27, 29, 32, 33, 45, 51
Malone, 69
Mandan, 93
Mangum, 99
Manistee, 83
Manitowoc, 47, 83
Manly, 99
Marietta, 67, 75
Marion, 71
Marmarth, 103
Marquette, 47, 103
Maryland, 11, 13, 15, 17, 19, 21, 23, 22, 25, 27, 29, 32, 33, 45, 51, 65, 67, 69, 73, 83, 85, 121
Marysvale, 113
Marysville, 87
Mason City, 101, 103
Massachusetts, 11, 13, 15, 17, 19, 21, 22, 25, 27, 29, 32, 33, 45, 51, 69, 104, 121
Matagorda, 91
Mattoon, 77
Maybrook, 67, 104
Maysville, 75
Mc Allister, 99
McCook, 59
McFarland, 47
McGehee, 107
McLeansboro, 75
Memphis, 15, 17, 21, 22, 27, 37, 39, 41, 49, 53, 57, 61, 73, 75, 77, 99, 107, 109, 119, 123
Mendenhall, 77
Menominee, 103
Meridian, 73, 77, 109
Mexico, 109
Miami, 81, 123
Michigan, 15, 17, 19, 21, 22, 25, 27, 29, 32, 33, 45, 47, 51, 67, 69, 83, 101, 103, 115, 121
Michigan City, 115
Midlesboro, 75
Miles City, 102
Milwaukee, 15, 17, 21, 27, 37, 39, 41, 47, 49, 53, 57, 61, 83, 103, 119, 123
Mina, 89
Minco, 47
Minneapolis, 35, 47, 93, 95, 97, 99, 101, 103, 123
Minnesota, 21,25, 27, 29, 32, 33, 35, 45, 47, 51, 77, 93, 95, 97, 99, 101, 103
Minnesota Territory, 17, 22
Minocqua, 47, 103
Minot, 95
Minster, 115
Mississippi, 15, 17, 21, 22, 25, 27, 29, 32, 33, 45, 51, 73, 75, 77, 107, 109
Mississippi River, 11, 22
Mississippi Territory, 11
Missoula, 122
Missouri, 15, 17, 19, 21, 23, 22, 25, 27, 29, 32, 33, 35, 45, 47, 51, 59, 75, 87, 89, 91, 97, 99, 103, 107, 109, 111
Mitchell, 103
Miwaukee, 101
Moberly, 111

Mobile, 21, 27, 37, 39, 41, 49, 53, 57, 61, 73, 75, 109, 119
Mojave, 91
Monarch, 113
Monroe, 77, 81
Montana, 33, 35, 51, 86, 92, 94, 97, 102
Montana Territory, 28, 32, 44
Montgomery, 15, 17, 21, 27, 37, 39, 41, 49, 53, 57, 61, 75, 79, 81, 109, 119, 123
Montrose, 113
Montréal, 69, 121
Moscow, 86, 94
Mounds, 113
Mount Shasta, 89
Mount Vernon, 75, 107
Muncie, 83, 115
Murphy, 73
Murphysboro, 109
Muskegon, 67, 83
Muskogee, 111
Myrtlewood, 75

Naples, 79
Nashville, 11, 15, 19, 21, 25, 27, 29, 37, 39, 41, 49, 53, 57, 61, 75, 119, 123
Natchez, 107
Nebraska, 32, 33, 35, 44, 47, 51, 59, 77, 87, 89, 97, 99, 101, 103, 107
Nebraska Territory, 21, 25, 27, 29
Needles, 91
Nelson, 47
Nevada, 28, 32, 33, 35, 44, 51, 60-61, 86, 89
New Bedford, 105
New Canaan, 104
New Hampshire, 11, 13, 15, 17, 19, 21, 22, 25, 27, 29, 32, 33, 45, 51, 69, 121
New Haven, 15, 17, 19, 21, 27, 49, 53, 57, 61, 104, 119, 123
New Jersey, 11, 13, 15, 17, 19, 21, 22, 23, 25, 27, 29, 32, 33, 45, 51, 65, 67, 69, 71, 105, 121
New Lisbon, 103
New London, 105
New Mexico, 33, 35, 89, 91, 97, 99, 113
New Mexico Territory, 28, 32, 44, 51
New Orleans, 11, 15, 17, 21, 22, 27, 35, 37, 39, 41, 49, 53, 57, 61, 73, 75, 77, 89, 107, 109, 119, 123
New York, 11, 13, 15, 17, 19, 21, 22, 25, 27, 29, 33, 45, 51, 65, 67, 69, 71, 83, 105, 115, 121
New York City 11, 15, 17, 19, 21, 23, 25, 27, 32, 37, 39, 41, 49, 53, 57, 61, 65, 67, 69, 71, 105, 119, 121, 123
Newark, 65
Newberry, 69
Newberry Jc., 71
Newport News, 83, 123
Newton, 123
Niagara Falls, 83
Nogales, 89
Norfolk, 25, 67, 73, 79, 81, 83, 85, 123
Norlina, 81
North Carolina, 11, 13, 15, 17, 19, 21, 22, 25, 27, 29, 32, 33, 45, 51, 73, 75, 79, 81, 85
North Dakota, 33, 35, 47, 51, 93, 95, 97, 101, 103
North Platte, 87
Northampton, 104
Norton, 75, 84

Oakdale, 91
Oakes, 47, 101
Oakland, 89, 122
Ogden, 35, 86, 89, 113, 122
Ogdensburg, 69
Ohio, 13, 15, 17, 19, 21, 22, 23, 25, 27, 29, 32, 33, 45, 51, 65, 67, 69, 71, 73, 75, 83, 85, 115, 121
Ohio River, 22
Oil City, 69
Okeechobee, 81
Oklahoma, 35, 47, 51, 89, 91, 97, 99, 107, 111
Oklahoma City, 91, 99, 111, 123
Olean, 67
Olympia, 86-87

Omaha, 35, 47, 59, 77, 87, 89, 97, 99, 101, 103, 107, 123
Oneida, 103
Ontagon, 47
Ontonagon, 103
Orange, 73, 83
Oregon, 28, 32, 33, 35, 44, 51, 86, 89, 92, 94
Orestod, 113
Orlando, 81, 123
Ortonville, 47
Osawatomie, 107
Ottawa, 69
Ottumwa, 103
Owensboro, 75, 77

Paducah, 75, 77, 97
Palatka, 73
Pamplin, 85
Paragould, 107
Paris, 69, 91
Parkersburg, 65
Parsons, 111
Pecos, 91
Pekin, 91
Pendleton, 86
Pennsylvania, 11, 13, 15, 17, 19, 21, 22, 23, 25, 27, 29, 32, 33, 45, 51, 65, 67, 69, 71, 83, 85, 115, 121
Pensacola, 75
Peoria, 47, 67, 69, 77, 97, 99, 101, 109, 115, 123
Peru, 83
Petersburg, 17, 81, 85
Petoskey, 83
Philadelphia, 15, 17, 19, 21, 23, 27, 37, 39, 41, 49, 53, 57, 65, 67, 119, 121, 123
Phoebus, 83
Phoenix, 89, 91, 122
Pierre, 47, 101
Pikeville, 83
Pittsburgh, 11, 23, 15, 19, 21, 22, 27, 37, 39, 41, 49, 53, 57, 61, 65, 67, 69, 119, 121, 123
Pittsfield, 104
Platte, 103
Plymouth, 83
Pocatello, 86
Pomeroy, 83
Poplar Bluff, 107
Port Boca Grande, 81
Port Huron, 83
Port Lewis, 71
Port Royal, 79
Portage, 103
Portland, 15, 17, 21, 27, 35, 37, 39, 41, 49, 52, 56, 60, 86, 89, 92, 94, 118, 122
Portsmouth, 17, 65, 81, 84
Posco, 122
Poughkeepsie, 104
Prescott, 91
Presidio, 91
Prince, 83
Promontory Point, 35
Providence 17, 21, 27, 49, 53, 57, 61, 105, 119, 123
Provo, 86, 89
Pueblo, 35, 47, 91, 97, 107, 113
Putnam, 105

Quincy, 47, 105

Racine, 103
Raleigh, 17, 73, 81, 123
Rapid City, 101
Raton, 91
Ravenna, 75
Reno, 89, 122-123
Rhode Island, 11, 13, 15, 17, 19, 21, 22, 25, 27, 29, 32, 33, 45, 51, 69, 105, 121
Richmond, 11, 15, 17, 19, 21, 27, 29, 37, 39, 41, 49, 53, 57, 61, 67, 73, 79, 81, 83, 85, 119, 123
Ridgway, 113
Rincon, 91
Roanoke, 84
Rochester, 65, 69, 123

Rock Island, 51, 99, -123
Rockford, 77
Rocky Mount, 79
Romulus, 83
Ronceverte, 83
Roodhouse, 109
Rosedale, 77
Rotan, 111
Rushville, 115
Ruskin, 99
Russell, 83
Rutherfordton, 81
Rutland, 15, 17, 21, 27, 49, 52, 56, 60, 118

Sacramento, 21, 27, 35, 89, 91, 122
Safe arbor, 123
Saginaw, 83
Saint Cloud, 95, 123
Saint Joseph, 21, 27, 37, 39, 41, 47, 49, 53, 57, 61, 87, 91, 97, 99, 107, 119
Saint Louis, 15, 19, 21, 22, 23, 25, 27, 37, 39, 41, 47, 49, 53, 57, 61, 65, 67, 69, 73, 75, 77, 89, 97, 99, 107, 109, 111, 115, 119, 121, 123
Saint Maries, 102
Saint Marys, 115
Saint Paul, 35, 47, 93, 95, 97, 99, 101, 103
Saint Petersburg, 123
Saint Thomas, 69, 83
Salem, 107
Salida, 113
Salina, 47, 87, 91, 107
Salinas, 122
Salisbury, 73, 123
Salt Lake City, 37, 39, 41, 49, 52, 56, 60, 86, 113, 118, 122
San Angelo, 91
San Antonio, 89, 107, 111, 123
San Bernardino, 86, 91
San Diego, 89, 91, 122
San Francisco, 35, 37, 39, 41, 49, 52, 56, 60, 89, 91, 118, 122
Sand Point, 122
Sandusky, 17, 65, 67, 115
Santa Barbara, 122
Santa Fe, 35, 39, 41, 49, 52, 56, 60, 91, 118
Santa Rosa, 99
Sardinia, 84
Savannah, 15, 17, 21, 27, 29, 37, 39, 41, 49, 53, 57, 60, 73, 79, 81, 119, 123
Scranton, 71
Searcy, 99
Seaside, 92
Seattle, 35, 39, 41, 49, 52, 56, 60, 86, 92, 94, 102, 118, 122
Sedalia, 107
Selma, 73, 75
Shawneetown, 65
Sheboygan, 101
Sheffield, 75
Shelby, 94
Shelton, 92
Shenandoah, 85
Sheriden, 47
Shreveport, 35, 77, 89, 107
Sierra Blanca, 89
Silman, 77
Silverton, 113
Sioux City, 77, 95, 97, 101, 103
Sioux Falls, 77, 95, 99
Skykomish, 94
Slater, 109
Sodus Point, 67
Soldier Summit, 113
Somerville, 91
Sonora, 91
South Bend, 67, 69
South Carolina, 11, 13, 15, 17, 21, 22, 25, 27, 29, 32, 33, 45, 51, 73, 75, 79, 81
South Dakota, 35, 47, 51, 77, 93, 95, 97, 99, 101, 103
Southern Erie, 51
Spanish Florida, 11

Spartanburg, 73, 79
Spencer, 103
Spokane, 35, 39, 41, 49, 52, 56, 60, 86, 92, 94, 102, 118, 122
Springfield, 17, 65, 77, 104, 109, 123
Stamford, 104
State Line, 104
Stockton, 91
Streator, 47, 69
Stuttgart, 99
Suffern, 71
Suffolk, 85
Sumas, 92, 102
Summit, 94
Sumter, 81
Superior, 91, 93, 95, 101, 103
Sweetwater, 91
Syracuse, 69, 123

Tacoma, 92, 102
Tallahassee, 25, 81
Tamms, 109
Tampa, 79, 81, 123
Taunton, 105
Teague, 99
Templc, 91, 123
Tennessee, 11, 15, 17, 19, 21, 22, 25, 27, 29, 32, 33, 45, 51, 73, 75, 77, 84, 107, 109
Terre Haute, 67, 103
Territory northwest of the Ohio River, 11
Territory south of the Ohio River, 11
Texarkana, 107
Texas, 21, 25, 27, 29, 32, 33, 35, 44, 51, 89, 91, 97, 99, 107, 111
Texline, 97
Thristle, 113
Tipton, 115
Toledo, 17, 21, 27, 49, 53, 57, 61, 65, 67, 69, 83, 115, 119, 121, 123
Topeka, 47, 87, 91, 99, 107, 123
Traverse City, 83
Trenton, 15, 17, 21, 27, 49, 53, 57, 61, 119
Trinidad, 113
Troy, 69
Tucson, 122
Tucumcari, 89, 99
Tulsa, 91
Tuscaloosa, 75
Tuscumbia, 17

Umatilla, 86
Union, 109
Union City, 75
Union Pacific, 35
Unorganized Territory, 21, 25, 27, 32, 33, 44
Utah, 33, 35, 86, 89, 113
Utah Territory, 28, 32, 44, 51
Utica, 69, 123

Valdosta, 73, 123
Vancouver, 94
Venice, 81
Vermont, 11, 13, 15, 17, 19, 21, 22, 25, 27, 29, 32, 33, 45, 51, 69, 121,
Vicksburg, 15, 17, 21, 27, 37, 39, 41, 49, 53, 57, 61, 77, 119
Vidalia, 81
Vincennes, 11, 65, 67
Vinita, 111
Virginia, 11, 13, 15, 17, 19, 21, 22, 23, 25, 27, 29, 32, 33, 45, 51, 65, 67, 73, 75, 79, 81, 83, 85

Waco, 111
Wadesboro, 79
Waldo, 81
Walla Walla, 86
Wallace, 86
Walsenburg, 113
Walton, 84-85
Washington, 33, 35, 51, 86, 89, 92, 102

Washington D. C., 11, 13, 15, 17, 19, 21, 27, 29, 37, 39, 41, 49, 53, 57, 61, 65, 67, 73, 83, 85, 119, 121, 123
Washington Territory, 28, 32, 44
Water Valley, 77
Waterbury, 104
Waterloo, 77
Watertown, 47
Waxahachie, 123
Waycross, 79
Wayne, 84
Waynoka, 91
Weehawken, 69
Weldon, 29
Wellington, 47
Wells, 86
Wenatchee, 94
Wendover, 97
West Jefferson, 84
West Lake Wales, 81
West Liberty, 47
West Palm Beach, 81, 123
West Point, 73
West Virginia, 29, 32, 33, 45, 51, 65, 67, 69, 73, 75, 83, 85, 115, 121
West Yellowstone, 86
Westport, 103
Wheeling, 19, 29, 65, 67, 115
Whitefish, 94
Wichita, 91, 99, 107, 123
Wichita Falls, 97, 111
Wildwood, 81, 123
Wilkes-Barre, 67
Willard, 65
Williamson, 84
Williamsport, 67
Williston, 95, 122
Willmor, 94-95
Wilmington, 11, 15, 17, 21, 27, 29, 37, 39, 41, 49, 53, 57, 61, 65, 79, 81, 119
Winchester, 67, 75
Winnemucca, 89
Winnipeg, 93
Winston-Salem, 73, 79, 84
Wisconsin, 17, 19, 21, 22, 25, 27, 29, 32, 33, 35, 45, 47, 51, 59, 77, 83, 93, 95, 97, 101, 103
Wisconsin Territory, 15
Wishram, 92, 94
Wood, 101
Woods Hole, 105
Woodville, 77
Worcester, 17, 21, 27, 49, 52-53, 56-57, 61, 105, 119, 123
Wyeville, 101
Wynne, 107
Wyoming, 33, 35, 47, 51, 86, 89, 92, 97, 101, 102
Wyoming Territory, 32, 44

Yakima, 86-87, 122
Yazoo, 77
York, 73
Youngstown, 69, 71
Yulee, 81
Yuma, 89, 122

Zanesville, 115

ACKNOWLEDGMENTS

Pictures are reproduced by permission of, or have been provided by the following:

Albany Institute of History and Art: 12.
Association of American Railroads: 20, 33 top, 33 bottom, 71, **98**.
Author's collection: 23, 36, 56.
Baltimore & Ohio Railroad: 14 top, 15 bottom, 19, 38, 43, 60, **64, 72**.
Chicago & North Western Railroad: 100.
Chicago, Quincy & Burlington Railroad: 58.
CSX Transportation: 82, 128.
Currier & Ives: 94.
Erie Railroad: 110.
ET Archive: front cover, 34, 70, 120.
Harper's Illustrated Weekly: 24.
Illinois Central Railroad: 50, 54, 87, 117.
Library of Congress: 30, 31.
Metropolitan Museum of Art, Bequest of Moses Tanenbaum, **1937: 104**.
Missouri Pacific Railroad: 106.
National Gallery of Art: 16.
New York Central System: 68, 90.
Norfolk Southern Corporation: 125 top.
Pennsylvania Railroad: 66.
Smithsonian Institution: 62.
Southern Pacific Lines: 88.
Union Pacific Railroad: 50, 54, 87, 117.
University of North Carolina Press: 125 bottom.
Virginia Museum of Transportation: 14 bottom, 15 top, 26 top, **28, 32, 39, 60,** 62, 119, 121.
West Virginia State Archives: 124.

Maps are based on data previously produced for:

Handbook of American Railroads (1951) by Robert G. Lewis:
67, 69, 71, 73, 75, 79, 81, 83, 85, 87, 89, 91, 93, 95, 97, 99, **101, 103, 105,** 107, 109, 111, 113, and 115.
Author's collection: 19, 29, 32, 33, 51, 57, 65, 77.

Design and Cartography: Elsa Gibert and Malcolm Swanston (**Arcadia** Editions Limited).